Individualizing
the
System

Dyckman W. Vermilye, EDITOR

1976

CURRENT ISSUES IN HIGHER EDUCATION

ASSOCIATE EDITOR, *William Ferris*

INDIVIDUALIZING
THE
SYSTEM

 Jossey-Bass Publishers
San Francisco · Washington · London · 1976

INDIVIDUALIZING THE SYSTEM
Dyckman W. Vermilye, Editor

Library of Congress Catalogue Card Number LC 76-11947

International Standard Book Number ISBN 0-87589-288-4

Manufactured in the United States of America

JACKET DESIGN BY WILLI BAUM

FIRST EDITION

Code 7614

THE JOSSEY-BASS SERIES IN HIGHER EDUCATION

 A publication of the

AMERICAN ASSOCIATION FOR HIGHER EDUCATION
National Center for Higher Education
One Dupont Circle, Northwest
Washington, D.C. 20036

DYCKMAN W. VERMILYE, *Executive Director*

The American Association for Higher Education, AAHE,
seeks to clarify and help resolve critical issues
in postsecondary education through conferences,
publications, and special projects. Its membership
includes faculty, students, administrators, trustees,
public officials, and interested citizens from all
segments of postsecondary education. This diversity
of membership reflects AAHE's belief that unilateral
solutions to problems are not as sound as those arrived
at through a coming together of all who are affected
by a problem.

Preface

Two themes weave their way through this book. One concerns the related concepts of quality and equality in our postsecondary education world. The concepts are relatively easy to identify—and celebrate—as separate, independent values. The trick comes in getting them to work together, for as Warren Bryan Martin states in the introduction to this volume, "We know that ideally these two values belong together, that the institution of higher education can go forward only by walking on both of these legs."

The second theme is human development. This theme, which is the central focus of Part One, grows out of a concern about recent trends toward bigger institutions, bigger systems, and (perhaps an inevitable consequence of bigness) management by the numbers. Preoccupied with cost efficiency, economies of scale, and systems theory, colleges may have drifted away from the mission of helping each student become a better, more complete human being. Concern for the system may have preempted concern for the individuals in it.

K. Patricia Cross suggests that we replace our goal of education for all with the goal of education for each. For Howard Bowen, the goal of educating people one by one is seen not as a new idea but as an essential feature of the university—a feature long recognized but lately lost sight of. A university, he argues, is more like a family or a work of art than a factory. Consequently, what is good about a university cannot easily be measured in numbers. For Bowen, as for Alison Bernstein, "college" is not just a place but a qualitative experience, and the richness of the experience depends on whether the campus environment stimulates or stifles individual growth. Bernstein poses a provocative series of questions about whether education can be meaningful on campuses that grow beyond certain dimensions of size. Her "diseconomies-of-scale" scale is likely to be remembered—and debated—whenever the question of size, quality, and equality is discussed.

In Part Two, human development is discussed in terms of faculty—or, more broadly, professional—development. Although the emphasis is on the improvement of teachers and teaching, the implications for student growth and development are obvious. Jerry Gaff offers a concise assessment of the state of the art in faculty development, and the remaining chapters of Part Two deal with specific aspects of the faculty development movement. Those less familiar with faculty development should find this section a useful introduction to the subject. Those with more familiarity will find it useful as a handbook of helpful hints.

Part Three deals with the question of money—as it affects institutions, as it affects students, and as it affects quality and equality in higher education. For many educators, the word *money* has vulgar connotations. They find it easier to speak of *finances,* of *support,* of *grants,* or of *funding.* It is unpleasant to think that educational practices are affected by the same stuff used to bet on horses or buy washing machines. Yet institutions lobby for that stuff, some fold for lack of it, faculty bargain for it, and students wonder whether they will make enough of it when they get a degree to compensate for the amount they and their parents sacrificed to get the degree. The money question may be a crass, vulgar question, but it is nevertheless a very real one, and the authors of Part Three consider its influence and potential influence on institutional survival and student choice.

The concluding section of the book deals with the ostensible commitment of higher education to equal opportunity and with the growing ambivalence within higher education concerning that commitment. Interestingly—and appropriately—the two authors who offer the most critical assessment of this ambivalence are not themselves academics. Eleanor Holmes Norton is a black, female, New York City public official, and Noel Epstein is a white, male, *Washington Post* education editor. Their complaints against higher education are strikingly similar. When two critics, writing from different perspectives, reach the same conclusions, their words bear heeding. Even more astonishing than the parallel between their arguments is the fact that both authors conclude with a question—in essence the same question: If America cannot find the answers it needs by turning to higher education, where can it turn? The question is more than a rhetorical ploy. It is a challenge.

My thanks to Dick Martin, who not only served as chairman of the planning group for the 31st National Conference on Higher Education, but who also helped select the conference papers to be included in this book and wrote the introductory essay. Thanks also to Howard Bowen, then president of the American Association for Higher Education, who also helped in the process of selecting papers for this volume. And, finally, thanks to Bill Ferris of the AAHE staff whose dependably deft hand at editing was added to his thoughtful estimate of the papers that ultimately were selected for this volume.

Washington, D.C.   Dyckman W. Vermilye
July 1976

Contents

TWO: IMPROVING TEACHERS AND TEACHING

THREE: THE MONEY QUESTION

FOUR: THE KNOCKING OF OPPORTUNITY

Contents

Contributors

Stephen K. Bailey, vice president, American Council on Education

Alison R. Bernstein, program officer, Fund for the Improvement of Postsecondary Education, Department of Health, Education and Welfare

J. Herman Blake, Provost of College VII, Oakes College, University of California, Santa Cruz

Howard R. Bowen, Avery professor of economics and education, Claremont Graduate School

Janet Welsh Brown, director of Opportunities in Science, American Association for the Advancement of Science

K. Patricia Cross, senior research psychologist, Educational Testing Service, and research educator, Center for Research and Development in Higher Education, University of California, Berkeley

Benjamin DeMott, professor of English literature, Amherst College

Noel Epstein, education editor, *The Washington Post*

Jerry G. Gaff, project director, Project on Institutional Renewal Through the Improvement of Teaching

Richard Gambino, associate professor of educational philosophy and director of the Italian-American studies program, Queens College, City University of New York

Timothy S. Healy, president, Georgetown University

Engin I. Holmstrom, research policy associate, American Council on Education

Morris Keeton, vice president and provost, Antioch College

Juanita M. Kreps, vice president and James B. Duke professor of economics, Duke University

Warren Bryan Martin, vice president, Danforth Foundation

Myron A. Marty, professor of history, Florissant Valley Community College

George J. Nolfi, president, University Consultants, Inc.

Donald M. Norris, assistant director, Office of Institutional Studies, University of Texas, Austin

Eleanor Holmes Norton, commissioner, New York Commission on Human Rights, New York City

H. Bradley Sagen, professor of higher education, College of Education, University of Iowa

Ronald W. Saufley, executive assistant to the provost of College VII, Oakes College, University of California, Santa Cruz

John R. Silber, president, Boston University

M. Elizabeth Tidball, professor of physiology, George Washington University Medical Center

George B. Weathersby, associate professor of education, Graduate School of Education, Harvard University

Individualizing
the
System

Equality and Quality: An Introduction

Warren Bryan Martin

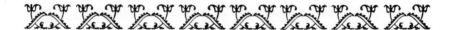

Although a growing number of Western intellectuals warn us of the need to escape from dichotomous, Cartesian modes of thinking—I/it, man/nature, normal/sick, black/white— the fact of the matter is that we seem consigned to think in opposites. We set things off against each other, even when we know that the proper goal should be to bring them together. We want to separate and define first, with the hope that later on we can blend and synthesize. We agree with the Jesuits: "Distinguish in order to unify." Our predilection for dualism and the "either/or" mode of thinking are employed even when the goal is a "both/and" objective.

This human tendency may be seen in a pair of opposites with which all of us must contend these days. I refer to education's joint commitment to equality and quality. We know that ideally these two values belong together, that the institution

1

of higher education in America can go forward only by walking on both of these legs. Equality without quality, or quality without equality, cripples the institution, stops its progress, leaves it maimed. Yet, influenced by the social division in the nation, as well as by the habitual way we organize our thinking, educators have tended to separate these concepts and to emphasize one rather than the other, or to put the stress first on one and then on the other.

Quality, some would have us believe, is a finite commodity, limited and scarce because of differences in human ability, interest, and motivation. They believe an unqualified commitment to quality necessitates a qualified commitment to equality. The chance to achieve quality should be equally distributed, but the actual achievement of it is destined to be unequal. To be concerned for quality is to be discriminating.

Equality, others insist, is the first priority for the educational community. Unlimited and bountiful, it permits a full realization of human potential. Achievement of quality must await equality of opportunity. Assure equality and, given human curiosity, ability, and energy, quality will follow. Trust human capabilities. If necessary, remove arbitrary standards and redefine criteria of excellence in order to give people a chance. Let broad-ranging equality of opportunities be accompanied by qualitative achievements of many forms. In the end, nontraditional forms of success may generate sufficient confidence that the people will proceed to acquire those skills necessary for traditional forms of success. To be concerned for equality is to be humane.

The problems created by setting quality and equality in opposition to one another are compounded by the tendency of educators to equate quality with elitism and equality with egalitarianism. Elitism is based no longer on fortuitous birth or social station but on individual accomplishment, on hard work and grit. In theory at least, and more and more in practice, honor goes to the meritocratic elite. The egalitarians, for their part, who in the recent past seemed obligated by unbending ideology to scorn almost all qualitative differentiation in education, are now acknowledging the invariability, if not the inevitability, of standards. There are, shall we say, meritocratic egalitarians.

A further complication is that this identification of quality with elitism and equality with egalitarianism, despite the accommodations previously mentioned, is carried into all aspects of professional life. For example, an educator's institutional affiliation is taken as prima facie evidence of his or her location in one or another of these ideological camps. Faculty and administrators from the established colleges and universities are presumed to be guardians of tradition, meaning elitism and quality. Persons at the newer places are presumed to be advocates of radical change, meaning egalitarianism and equality.

All of this leads to the conclusion that the major division in higher education is not between the public and private sectors, nor between professional training and liberal learning, but is in fact between the meritocratic elite and the social egalitarians, with the first faction waving the flag of "quality" and the second sounding the trumpet of "equality." Such a division is serious, not so much because of the differentiation in functions, but precisely because quality and equality are thereby separated. That which the democratic ideal could bring together, the pragmatic realists would put asunder.

It was Thomas Jefferson who first pointed out in this country the connection between education and a free society: "If a nation expects to be ignorant and free in a state of civilization," wrote Jefferson, "it expects what never was and never will be." And there has been an unbroken line of influence from Jefferson to Horace Mann, for whom the schools and schooling held the key to all human progress, to John Dewey, who talked about the schools as society's instrument for shaping its own destiny, to the present confidence despite recent setbacks that makes the school, as D. W. Brogan said, "America's formally unestablished national church."[1]

There were, as we know, hidden and unexamined assumptions in this tradition that gave to the notion of equality of opportunity a limited application. Jefferson wanted equality of educational opportunity in Virginia and, in pursuit of this objective, helped to establish the University of Virginia. But Jefferson's equality extended only to the sons of free white fam-

[1]D. W. Brogan, *The American Character* (New York: Vintage Books, 1956).

ilies. The problem has always been that some people are more equal than others.

No less important has been the historic connection between education, including higher education, and the sociopolitical status quo. John Dewey's educational philosophy was shaped by and brought to the service of the social organization of industrial technology and the political ideology of competitive capitalism. Educators have been agents of politics and socialization, and have used education as an instrumentality of control to perpetuate class distinctions. Furthermore, we need not become Marxists to become disabused of a central idea of political liberalism—that education is, or can be, the solvent of social ills in a capitalist economy. From the days of John Stuart Mill, this has been the claim of liberal reformers. Education is not only to be esteemed as a way to self-development, but as the peaceful and relatively painless equalizer of social and economic disparities.

It is the differential application of equality by those who profess to be concerned for standards that infuriates the social egalitarians. They are also angered by the use of quality education to perpetuate social inequities. Yet the egalitarians on campus seem to accept education as the way to effect social and political transformation as well as the answer to the needs of the individual. They too put their faith in education.

Social egalitarians in higher education draw their theory from Rousseau and Marx and, very recently, from Rawls. From Rousseau they derive the idea that a citizen has no rights that do not coincide with the "General Will." But the complexity of modern society makes any viable connection with the simple agrarianism of Rousseau tenuous and forced. The connection with Marx is based on the Marxist claim that the inevitable next step in social and economic development is the classless society. Yet Marx's formula, "to each according to his need" is not "to each the same." And in Russia, from the time of Lenin, who relied on a meritocratic elite, to the present, when the Party represents a self-conscious elite, social egalitarianism has not been achieved.

De Tocqueville foresaw that under democracy the movement would be from equality before the law to equality in economic well-being, from equality of opportunity to equality of achievement, from rights to results. And the theory or rationale for that evolving position has been given strong expression by John Rawls. The primary aim of society, argues Rawls, is justice defined as fairness, and fairness means equality—not just equality of opportunity but equality of condition. Instead of accepting the unequal distribution of rewards determined by a market economy, society should accept the "principle of redress." Equality of opportunity is a delusion and an evil unless it produces equality of results. Hence, to produce genuine equality of opportunity, society must give more attention to those persons born into less favorable social positions.[2]

In American colleges and universities, there are now many faculty and students who are hostile to competition in teaching and learning because it discriminates, particularly against those persons who have been at a disadvantage in acquiring the attitudes and skills necessary to succeed under the pressure of such competition. Furthermore, competition exposes people to the negative effects of discouragement when what they need is reinforcement. If there are to be procedures that separate, sort, and track, let them be structured to favor those who need a running start in order to keep pace. Equality precedes quality.

Elitists are concerned that excellence be recognized, fostered, and rewarded. There are irreducible differences in ability, energy, and motivation, as well as in interests—differences qualitative as well as quantitative. It is not just that one person is best at doing one thing and somebody else better at another. As Anthony Quinton puts it, "Almost anyone can adequately remove garbage, load and unload trucks, work on an assembly line, clean the floors of office buildings. Rather few people can effectively perform brain operations, manage large industrial enterprises, play Hamlet, judge complex legal cases, investigate the fine structure of matter."[3] It is quality education and disciplined training, for people of ability and determination, that give society those essential services of the higher order.

---

[2]J. Rawls, *A Theory of Justice* (Cambridge, Mass.: Harvard University Press, 1971).

[3]A. Quinton, "Elitism: A British View," *The American Scholar, 44* (1975–1976): 727.

However technical, this is humanistic education because on it humanity's future depends.

One of the most persuasive arguments for the traditions of the humanistic educational ideal, with its elitist connotations, has been made by Lionel Trilling. He points out that for earlier generations of Western European people it was incentive enough for a person to have before him (yes, almost always "him") the goal of doing what his father had done, doing it as well or better—as a baker, or whatever. And there was, as a corollary, the notion of apprenticeship, of training in a skill that resulted in progression from novice to master. Today, particularly in America, the emphases have shifted. First, and most importantly, we insist on options—career options, options in location, work, and social relationships. We cannot bear being "located" because location carries with it the idea of being restricted, confined, or put in a fixed position. Moreover, the mood of immediacy is on us—immediate access, immediate gratification and progression, immediate success. The long, hard, sequential patterns of learning, growing, attaining over extended periods of time are now untenable. So, said Trilling, we are ill disposed to stay with a task, unwilling to pay the price. And, because discipline and dedication are essential to learning the humanistic ideal and to earning one's place in that tradition, we are more likely to surrender the tradition than to work for it.[4]

Do we agree with Trilling that quality will probably give way to equality and that in the process something essential to a democratic society will be lost? Is there such a thing as "equalitarian" education? The experience of the American city may possibly be replicated in higher education. A distinct bifurcation has taken place in our urban centers, with the inner city becoming the home of the poor and unskilled and the outer ring becoming the home of the rich and skilled. Despite efforts ranging from educational to economic, we are separating—by class and caste. A similar outcome is possible for education and educational institutions. "Academic" education could exist along with "educational" education. There could be narrowly aca-

[4]Trilling, "The Uncertain Future of the Humanistic Educational Ideal," *The American Scholar 44* (1974–1975): 1.

demic institutions and broadly educational ones. Quality would be set over against equality. The sons and daughters of the lower class would go, for the most part, to the egalitarian, broadly educational institutions, while the sons and daughters of the affluent go to the elitist, narrowly academic institutions. There would be something for everybody. But not everybody would have something equally valuable.

Can we be content to know that our solution to the tension between quality and equality is to arrange for some of our people to have the former and all of our people the latter? Quality without equality will constantly be under attack as alien to the achievement of social democracy. Hence, being contrary to the basic purpose of our society, its satisfaction can be only partial. Quality without equality is like baseball before the introduction of blacks. Jackie Robinson brought more than equality to baseball. He brought a new level of quality to the game.

As for equality without quality, it provides no means for its own perpetuation. How can equality be defined, extended, and improved if it is devoid of qualitative standards? Equality must assume the presence of quality or determine to achieve it. There is no way to ignore it. Alas, quality may endure without equality but equality cannot survive without quality.

The definitions of quality and equality are never static. We are constantly defining and achieving them. Furthermore, the core issue is not equality or quality, one versus the other, but how to relate them harmoniously. At this time in our history, Americans increasingly acknowledge the need for both. Some slight comfort may be taken from that considerable gain. But we tend to set one apart from the other. That fact is our embarrassment and our loss. There is no greater challenge to higher education in this bicentennial year than to bring together, to reconcile these two precious ideals, to recognize that only through equality of opportunity can we have diversity of achievement and only through that diversity can the quality of our achievements as a nation be enriched.

1

Where Numbers Fail

Howard R. Bowen

One of the classic passages on the nature of the university is Cardinal Newman's statement, "A university is . . . an Alma Mater, knowing her children one by one, not a foundry, or a mint, or a treadmill."[1] The same concept was expressed by John Dewey, who said, "What the best and wisest parent wants for his child, that must the community want for all its children. Any other ideal for our schools is narrow and unlovely; acted upon it destroys our democracy."[2]

In contrast with the spirit of these quotes, much of the planning for higher education today is strongly influenced by the point of view and the jargon of business management. Phrases such as *cost-benefit analysis, cost effectiveness, marginal cost analysis, systems analysis, accountability, market research, program budgeting, management by objectives,* and *computerized models for long-range projections* are commonplace in the discussions

[1] *The Scope and Nature of University Education* (New York: E. P. Dutton, 1958), p. 122.
[2] In R. D. Archambault (Ed.), *John Dewey on Education* (Chicago: University of Chicago Press, 1974), p. 295.

of planning, though less so in the actual practice of planning. The underlying assumption is that the techniques and the point of view of business planning are applicable to higher education. Some enthusiasts even argue that the financial problems of higher education would be resolved if only it would adopt sound, hard-headed, and rational business management procedures. This claim surely exaggerates the potential returns from any conceivable managerial technique.

I am somewhat skeptical about the management movement for higher education. I am even dubious about the use of the word *management,* which strikes me as alien to an organization that is essentially a community and that bears little resemblance to a profit-making business, a governmental bureau, or an army. This is not to say that I am opposed to planning for higher education. Rational planning to achieve efficiency is relevant to any human activity. But efficiency is not confined to results measured in money or to goods traded in a market. It applies to intangible goals such as personal serenity, artistic appreciation, and humane learning, as well as to the production of bread and gasoline.

My quarrel, then, is not with efficiency or planning for efficiency in higher education, but with planning in the style of business management that tends to focus on quantifiable variables *to the exclusion of other variables.* A further problem with such planning is that it assumes the presence of a management that has the power of command over the organization. Worthwhile academic planning will take into account *all* the benefits of a course of action and all the costs, not just those that are quantifiable. Any system of planning that counts enrollment as the sole output and counts cash outlays for institutions and student aid as the sole costs will at best be irrelevant and will at worst convert education into a treadmill (to quote Cardinal Newman), and may even destroy our democracy (to quote John Dewey). Educators should scrupulously resist the kind of planning, now being thrust on them by a multitude of outside pressures, that reduces everything to a few simple numbers. They should insist on looking squarely at the means and the ends in human terms.

The problem was not so serious in the simpler days when higher education was a modest enterprise and the relatively small single campuses enjoyed considerable autonomy. But today planning increasingly takes place in huge universities, complex multicampus institutions, statewide coordinating bodies, legislative committees, and state finance offices. Political and bureaucratic mentality is rapidly gaining influence. As a result, the tendency to think in narrow quantitative terms and to ignore the human dimensions of ends and means has become alarming.[3]

A useful analogy can be made between a college or university and a family. Like a college, a family is an environment in which people live, grow, and relate to one another. When we speak of efficiency for a family, we do not talk of credits earned, cost per person, ratio of parents to children, or index of space utilization. We judge the success of a family in terms of mutual affection, solidarity, helpfulness, willingness to sacrifice for one another, the aspirations and values of its members, its style of life, and the kinds of people it produces. The factors making for the success or failure of families are so subtle and intangible that they are almost indiscernible. We know a good family when we see one (though there may be differences of opinion in some cases), and we regard a good family more as a work of art than as the product of some standardized technology.

From a narrow, pecuniary point of view, the typical American family is grossly inefficient. It wastes housing space. It provides specialized rooms for sleeping, eating, work, and recreation that are unused most of each day. It prepares food in inefficiently small quantities. It operates two cars that sit in the garage or on a parking lot most of the time. The mother may refrain from joining the paid labor force. It caters to the special needs of its individual members and loses many of the economies of scale. We not only condone these inefficiencies, we applaud them by calling them a high standard of living. We do make judgments as to what constitutes an acceptable minimal family income, but we regard this amount as a necessary but not sufficient condition for achieving the intangible qualities

[3]See H. L. Enarson, "The Art of Planning," *Educational Record 56* (Summer 1975): 170–174; and I. R. Hoos, "The Costs of Efficiency," *Journal of Higher Education 46* (March/April 1975): 141–159. These two papers are strongly recommended.

of a good family. We recognize that the performance of families cannot be measured by money alone, and that the concept of efficiency for families has little kinship with efficiency for factories or government bureaus.

A college or university is very much like a family. It is a place where people are joined in common pursuits. It is designed for the personal development of people of all ages, for the preservation and advancement of learning and the arts, and directly and indirectly for the advancement of society. Production in higher education is concerned with bringing about desired characteristics in people and facilitating scholarly endeavor. A college or university does its work through creating the right environment. The visible attributes of that environment are an aggregation of land, buildings, equipment, and supplies, and a group of people including students, faculty, staff, and governing groups. The invisible environment is the campus culture, consisting of the prevailing ways of doing things, the common values, expectations, standards, assumptions, traditions, behavioral patterns, and an ineffable quality called *atmosphere*.

In the academic environment, the people involved—both students and faculty—not only draw from the environment but contribute to it as participants. They provide the role models, the peer groups, the experiences in interpersonal relations that are so significant in human development and in scholarly productivity. Their participation enhances the benefits they receive.

The goals of the academic environment are not specific objectives forced on people but are a broad range of opportunities people are free to accept and use in different ways. College is a place of stirring; it is a catalyst to help people find their unique ways, not a rigidly patterned system with preprogrammed outcomes for everyone; it gives each person the chance to work out his or her unique destiny in a setting that raises aspirations, permits exploration and experimentation, provides encouragement and support, and offers the chance to learn in both the cognitive and affective spheres. Similarly, the outcomes of research and public service activities are determined primarily by the interaction of the institutional environment with a faculty who have considerable latitude in choice of activities, subject matter, and procedures.

A good college or university, like a good family, is largely a work of art. The principles of production are only vaguely known except through tradition, intuition, and judgment. In the case of higher education, we do not even have a clear notion of what constitutes poverty or minimal adequacy of resources for achieving any particular mission. We operate our institutions with widely varied expenditures per student. For example, according to the Carnegie Commission, educational and general expenditures per student in a category of institutions as homogeneous as selective liberal arts colleges ranged in 1967–1968 from $900 to $5,900 (a difference of $5,000). And the range between the first and third quartiles was from $1,800 to $2,800 (a difference of $1,000 per student).[4] Similar differences were recorded among institutions of other categories. The presumption is that the expensive institutions are producing outcomes that are superior in some sense to those produced in the less expensive institutions, but no one can be sure that presumption is valid. We have even less clear notions as to how given resources should be deployed internally to produce the best results. In cynical moments, it is easy to believe that the whole higher educational enterprise is run on three crass principles: (1) each institution gets all the money it can raise; (2) it spends all the money it can get; and (3) its internal allocations are arranged on the basis of incremental annual adjustments based on external and internal political pressures.

In view of our monumental ignorance, one must ask whether academic planning is possible at all in the strict sense of measuring the means and the ends. The condition of our industry certainly suggests the need for more knowledge about the relation between the resources and technologies employed and the true outcomes in human terms. I see the exploration of these relationships as the primary task of those who would improve rational planning in higher education. Without adequate knowledge in these areas, which will require decades of research, higher education will remain dependent on tradition, intuition, and judgment for guidance in its decision making. I do not deprecate tradition, intuition, and judgment. These are

[4]Carnegie Commission on Higher Education, *New Students and New Places* (New York: McGraw-Hill, 1971), pp. 70–80.

our only sources of wisdom in most of the important matters of life—for example, love, friendship, religion, morality, beauty, personal life-style, and foreign policy. But in higher éducation it would be useful to know a bit more about the relationship of our decisions and actions to our goals.

In the absence of precise knowledge about that relationship, how can the actual decision-making process be carried out in higher education? We are all aware of the constraints imposed by external and internal pressures. The president is often described as the mediator among a multitude of pressure groups. This description applies especially to presidents of institutions that are largely governed by formulas imposed by external public bodies. But to the extent that autonomy remains, presidents and their close associates can be leaders. They can amass considerable power in league with their administrative colleagues and boards; they can win faculty, student, and public support for significant plans; and they can effect these plans through timely, astute, incremental action. Even in those institutions where autonomy is minimal, presidents and their associates can influence the external governing body. But leadership can be effective only if it is based on a coherent long-range plan that in turn is founded on a sound educational philosophy. I cannot overemphasize the importance of the underlying philosophy. Such a plan may or may not be reduced to writing. In either case it should be flexible enough to allow for unexpected circumstances but not so flexible as to deny the philosophy on which it is based. It should provide specific opportunities for decisions leading to specific actions. It should serve as a road map that indicates the leader's destination, describes the best route to that destination, and traces out alternative paths if the main route should be blocked. The result of such planning and execution is the work of art to which I referred.

A good plan will avoid two frequent errors. The first, common to legislatures and economy-minded critics, is to judge efficiency only in relation to cost, on the assumption that any change in procedure that costs less, regardless of its effect on outcomes, is efficient. The second error, common to the proponents of higher education, is to judge efficiency only in relation to outcomes, on the assumption that any change in procedure that improves outcomes, regardless of cost, is desirable. Both of these approaches fail to recognize that efficiency is a relationship between two variables, cost and outcome, and cannot be measured by either one alone.

Let me offer some illustrations of institutional decision making in the context of a long-range plan. I do this to show how foreign most actual decision making is, and must be, from the so-called managerial approach to college administration.

My first example relates to the allocation of faculty among departments. Suppose opportunity has opened up to add a new professorship. The department of history is strong; the department of sociology is weak. Should the professorship be placed in sociology or history? The easy answer is sociology. But this answer implies that all departments should be of about equal academic strength, which may lead to a general mediocrity of the whole academic community. Would it not be better to convert history from a strong to a superb department on the principle that the effectiveness of the total academic community will be enhanced by developing some centers of exceptional academic strength even at the cost of holding other departments at lesser strength? The decision in favor of history would be clearer if a distinguished historian were available but not a sociologist of equal distinction. I am not trying to provide a solution to one concrete problem; I am only trying to cite a specific issue where the president is cast in the role of artist. His canvas is the total academic community. His artistic judgment is like that of a painter who is deciding on the strength of the red in a particular part of his canvas or like that of a symphony director who expresses his esthetic judgment in determining the tempo and the loudness of the brass section in a particular musical passage.

Let us take another illustration. The plan calls (in this case, secretly) for the elimination of several departments that are deemed obsolete and inessential. With the retirement of the last tenured professor in one of these departments, it is decided to act with respect to that department. The immediate uproar includes not only the remaining staff of the department but also the relevant national and state professional associations, alumni, the state legislature, and currently enrolled students. Added to the uproar is the voice of faculty members in vulnerable departments who suspect that their departments may be next. The question, then, is whether the leadership should push through a series of bloody battles year after year in order to prune several departments representing .5 percent of the budget? Would it be wiser to devote administrative energy to other more productive matters and achieve the budgetary saving in some other way—for example, by slowing up the increase in faculty salaries? Again, I do not answer the question. I only demonstrate that real life decisions are often judgmental. They are part of the process of producing a work of art. Sometimes dissonance is part of a musical composition.

Another example relates to elimination of faculty deadwood by withholding increases in salary and rank and by early retirement. The question here is one of fairness, humanity toward the people involved, and the effect on the morale of the younger faculty, who realize that someday they too will grow old. Is it better to put up with some deadwood or find useful and dignified things for the less creative people to do and thus maintain a secure and loyal faculty, or is it better to push such people out? Again I do not answer the question, I only point out that it calls for artistry in another part of the canvas.

My final example concerns buildings. How important educationally is it to have an esthetically satisfying campus with well-sited, well-designed buildings, pleasing landscapes, and attractive interiors? And how valuable is tidiness in building maintenance? On these matters, nonquantitative artistic judgments must be made about costs and outcomes. The same kinds of questions must be answered by academic leaders about building utilization, the size of classes, mechanized instruction, other new methods of teaching and learning, faculty teaching loads, admissions criteria, and a host of other matters. In each instance, the main task of planning is to implement a coherent philosophy of higher education that sets the general goals and results in a work of art.

One important task of the leadership is to communicate the plan to the academic community. The best way to do this is through a consistent pattern of decisions. Other devices are formal reports, informal memoranda, speeches, and casual comments in board and committee meetings or even at cocktail parties. Often, informal modes of communication are more effective than formal ones. The problem is continually to transmit signals through actions and words consistent with the plan.

Finally, a cautious attitude needs to be cultivated with respect to forecasting, which is an important part of the managerial approach to planning. No reasonable person can be averse to forecasting, provided the forecasts are not taken too seriously. The best assumption to make about the future is that it will bring surprises. For example, we do not know, for any given future date, whether the nation will be at war or at peace, in depression or prosperity, in inflation or deflation. We are in the dark about future attitudes of potential students toward higher education, their preferences for different courses of study, and their behavior patterns. Student decisions are highly volatile. We are ignorant about future public attitudes toward the support of higher education. We have only the vaguest notions about future demands of adult learners. We have no knowledge of future governmental programs that may have profound effects on enrollments, financial support, and the responsibilities of higher education.

Even this very year, enrollments in both the public and private sectors are far above expectations, and no one really knows why. A few months ago people were saying that the slack job market would discourage college attendance; now they are saying unemployment is the cause of the increased enrollment. Another illustration of sudden changes in student behavior occurred at the time of Cambodia and the Kent State affair. After the events of the spring of 1970, most educators had forebodings about the following fall. Yet, when autumn came, the students returned in a nonbelligerent and cooperative mood. These experiences suggest that academic leaders should be very cautious and humble about forecasts and projections. As an economist, I know from harsh experience how wrong forecasts and projections can be, how easy it is to overlook major variables, and how often one is confounded by surprises.

One of my economist friends has a sign in his office that reads, "Statistics are no substitute for judgment." In our present state of ignorance the best foundation for planning is a solid and consistent philosophy of education and steadfast adherence to that philosophy as events unfold and as decisions are made. The best approach to the improvement of planning is to learn more about the functional relations between resource inputs and technologies on the one hand and the outcomes in human terms on the other.

2

How Big Is Too Big?

Alison R. Bernstein

In 1900, the total number of students enrolled in higher education was 250,000. Now, three systems—the City University of New York, the State University of New York, and the California State system each have about a quarter of a million students. Approximately one third of all persons enrolled in postsecondary education attend institutions with more than 20,000 students. Why are contemporary American colleges and universities so large? Are massive institutions inevitable when society is committed to mass higher education? Or are we showing symptoms of what the British economist E. F. Schumacher calls the "idolatry of giantism?"[1]

Is giantism the price we pay for opening our colleges and universities to the masses? If we want to accommodate all who desire to attend some form of postsecondary education, must we continue to think that the only way to educate large numbers of students is in bigger but not necessarily better learning en-

[1]E. F. Schumacher, *Small Is Beautiful* (New York: Harper & Row. 1973), p. 21.

vironments? To arrive at a partial answer to the questions, we must understand how we got into this "bigger-is-better" bind in the first place. In the 1950s and 1960s, educational planners talked about economies of scale. (Unfortunately the majority still do despite the problems connected with this kind of solution.) Economies of scale minimize the cost per unit by maximizing the volume. If a faculty member lectures 60 students, why not have him or her lecture 600 students? Why have a president for 2,000 students when the same person, paid the same salary, can oversee an institution of 20,000?

Modeled along this line of reasoning, institutions were developed to "handle" unprecedented numbers of individuals. Administrations were centralized and administrators channeled into specialized roles. Faculty course loads were calculated on the basis of numbers of students taught, and facilities were designed to house and feed students with assembly-line efficiency. There is a production-oriented logic to this approach. If the purpose of bringing all these new students into college was to produce degrees at low cost, then one has to admit that the system worked.

Perhaps the most influential document to incorporate the economies-of-scale approach was the 1972 report, *The More Effective Use of Resources,* issued by the Carnegie Commission on the Future of Higher Education. Using economies of scale as the basis for its recommendations about institutional size, the Commission suggested that plans for growth and development should, "in general, incorporate *minimum* FTE [full-time equivalent] enrollment objectives of (1) 5,000 students for doctoral-granting institutions, (2) 5,000 students for comprehensive colleges, (3) 1,000 students for liberal arts colleges, and (4) 2,000 students for community colleges."[2] The purpose of these recommendations was to make administrators and trustees aware that institutions with enrollments below these figures, even if operating in the black, might be uneconomical. Carnegie also published maximum enrollment figures in each category. Institutions that grant Ph.D.s should not exceed 20,000 students, community colleges 5,000, and liberal arts institutions

[2]Carnegie Commission, *The More Effective Use of Resources* (New York: McGraw-Hill, 1972), p. 41.

2,500. These figures were based on three assumptions: "one, beyond these levels, no more savings in financial costs could be made; two, quality programs could be achieved certainly by these levels and finally, some disadvantages of size become more apparent after these limits are reached."[3]

Even if the Carnegie Commission's figures represent only approximate limits, many colleges and universities have exceeded the boundaries separating economies from *diseconomies* of scale. Also, within the boundaries indicated, little is known about the relationship of size to program quality. What if students want more from college than exposure to 120 credits and the acquisition of a credential? What if they want to learn how to learn and to experience personal growth? What if students desire more than an increased knowledge base? What impact does the *size* of a learning environment have on goals like these? Unfortunately, we know very little about the subject. Arthur Chickering has pointed out that "there has been little research that has attempted to study relationships between personal development and college size."[4]

Nevertheless, both Chickering and I have our own hypotheses about the effect of large institutions on individuals. Some of his hypotheses are based on research carried out in high school settings, which, he argues, may duplicate the problems of massive postsecondary institutions. One study, Barker and Gump's *Big School, Small School* (1964), found that as schools increase in size, the number of persons increases much faster than either the number of learning settings or the varieties of settings. Students in small schools held an average of 3.5 responsible positions per student; students in large schools averaged .5 responsible positions. Students in small schools were involved in more activities than those in large schools and had more satisfying experiences related to developing competence, being challenged, and engaging in important activities.[5] This study and the findings of others, Chickering asserts, "suggest a negative relationship between size, and individual participation, involvement and satisfaction."[6]

[3]Carnegie Commission, p. 212.
[4]A. Chickering. *Education and Identity* (San Francisco: Jossey-Bass, 1969), p. 185.
[5]Barker and Gump, as quoted in Chickering, p. 186.
[6]Chickering, p. 186.

Another study concerns the development of a congruent, coherent personality. W. J. Bowers discovered in his work on cheating that "The proportion of schools with high levels of cheating increased with the size of the school."[7] He observed that "at small schools, students tend to know most of their peers, whereas at large schools, they get to know only a fraction of the student body. Therefore, the student at the large school is apt to feel relatively anonymous vis-a-vis the student body as a whole. The large.schools may provide a setting that facilitates the formation of deviant subgroups in which cheating is approved or at least tolerated."[8] After reading about Bowers's study, I was reminded about the great term paper scandals at Boston University a couple of years ago. Could this kind of plagiarism have gone undetected for as long at a small institution where faculty and students have a more intimate knowledge of each other's activities?

To the small body of research concerning the impact of institutional size on student development, I'd like to add a couple of observations of my own from working at the Fund for the Improvement of Postsecondary Education. First, the massive size of a great many institutions stifles not only student development but the entire process of innovation. A careful review of the more than 2,000 proposals submitted during 1975–1976 suggests difficulties in both proposing and implementing new programs within the embedded bureaucracies of our large university systems. It is hard to bring to mind any proposals for bold innovation from multicampus systems. The amount of paperwork and the arduous process of getting a proposal approved for submission are enough to frustrate even the best and most creative educational innovators.

Second, after a proposal is funded, the process of change itself is often hindered in large institutions. Faculty members are usually unaware of the activities of their colleagues in other departments. A faculty development project at a small liberal arts college can be introduced for $25,000 in a summer workshop for the entire faculty. The communication alone in a large institution requires thousands of dollars. It is a massive prob-

[7]W. J. Bowers, *Student Dishonesty and Its Control in College* (New York: The Bureau of Applied Social Research, Columbia University, 1964), p. 123.
    [8]Bowers, p. 123.

lem in logistics. Although I have no empirical evidence to support it, my belief is that faculty at large institutions tend to be more cynical than their counterparts in small colleges. They sense their powerlessness over their working conditions; and faculty contracts, especially those developed as the result of collective bargaining, show that many faculty have given up exercising "ownership" of the institution. Their loyalties have shifted from their institutions to their disciplines and disciplinary associations. Not surprisingly, the frustrations, cynicism, and alienation of the faculty are reflected in the students. In the past couple of years, large institutions have turned to individualized instruction as one answer to the charge that they have ignored the needs of students as individuals. In its broadest sense, individualized instruction means a variety of new learning methodologies: personalized systems of instruction, competency-based education, computer-assisted instruction, experiential learning, and independent study. Although these techniques are quite different in process and approach, they all seek to customize learning to the individual student's abilities, skills, and goals. They recognize differences in learning rates among students as well as the validity of learning that occurs outside the classroom. In some ways, individualized instruction is an American adaptation of the tutorial model. The process is carried out in two ways: either students design their own course of study in conjunction with a faculty member (or sometimes two or three advisors) or the faculty member designs a course of study that can be mastered by students individually. In both processes, students are not constrained by time, previous preparation, or their fellow classmates.

Because individualized instruction is a constructive approach to the increasing heterogeneity of students, proposals employing individualized instruction have received considerable support from the Fund for the Improvement of Postsecondary Education. These programs offer solutions to a number of problems associated with returning adult students. Adults do not have to sit in lecture halls when they can master the same material at home or at a more convenient time. Adult programs award credit for learning that has occurred outside formal educational institutions. Without an individualized program, the higher education experience of many adults might be remembered only as an endless registration line followed by an endless series of lectures and capped by a graduation exercise in an auditorium the size of Madison Square Garden.

For some educators, individualized instruction does not go far enough to meet the needs of adults. They believe adults should be able to earn a degree without ever setting foot in a classroom. The Regents External Degree, established by the University of the State of New York, offers this kind of possibility. The Regents External Degree does not itself "educate" persons. It delivers no learning services and has no fulltime faculty, mentors, or learning facilitators. It does evaluate the education individuals have received elsewhere. The evaluation and assessment instruments of the Regents External Degree measure primarily cognitive learning, not individual development. An adult student's experiences with the Regents External Degree may be summed up as "the postman always rings twice—once to give you the forms and once to deliver your diploma."

Individualized instruction is also being touted as the answer to the problems of open admissions—what remains of it, that is. If students are not under pressure to master a course in a semester, or even a year, faculty can maintain standards without having to penalize students. The concept of a "revolving door," in which students are given access only to be told later that they cannot make the grade, would be eliminated. The pressures of time and competition can be reduced. Students are free to do as much or as little as they wish. Courses can be divided into manageable units of study. Students can sign "learning contracts" committing themselves to attain prescribed levels of competence. This individualized approach to the learning needs of low-achieving and disadvantaged students can be a meaningful way to accommodate a more ethnically and racially heterogeneous student population.

But is individualized instruction really an answer to the problems associated with size? We may have assumed so too quickly. In fact, increasing the individualization of instruction may intensify rather than ease an individual's sense of anomie, isolation, and discomfort within the system. Two years ago, Virginia Smith, the director of the Fund, warned that "much individualized instruction is more concerned with cognitive development than with affective growth . . . the present trends in development of Individualized Instruction do appear to exacerbate our present inadequacies to educate the whole person."[9] The educational experience may indeed become more fragmented through our increasing attention to individual learning. When a student once did not know other students in a large lecture hall, at least the lecture became a shared activity. Now, with each degree individualized and every unit modularized, a student finds it increasingly difficult to experience the common themes that might make learning socially coherent and meaningful. A nightmare of mine goes like this: to correct the problems of colleges with massive enrollments, we create individual self-contained learning vehicles that propel students in and out of institutions without their having to touch or be touched by anyone save perhaps a lone learning mentor. We combat institutional size by enhancing an individual's feeling of separateness from others. It's as if educational reform is capable only of bouncing from one extreme to the other.

Another reform that large systems are supporting in order to help individuals is consumer education. I find this new movement interesting and ironic. In effect, it is using the system to educate students to beat the system. Student consumers ought to know the truth behind the promises of a college catalogue. When do courses get oversubscribed? How long does it really take to complete a degree? The Fund has supported consumer education in much the same way it has supported individualizing instruction. During 1975–1976, grants were made to eleven institutions to develop an institutional prospectus that includes, among other things, "descriptions and explanations of student attrition and retention rates; types of students who are most productive at the institution; current student and faculty perceptions on the quality of the learning process; student-faculty interactions and the environment of the institution as viewed by various student sub-cultures."[10]

[9]V. Smith, "Individualized Self-Paced Instruction," in R. S. Ruskin and S. S. Bono (Eds.), *Personalized Instruction in Higher Education: Proceedings of the 1st National Conference* (Washington D.C.: The Center for Personalized Instruction, Georgetown University, April 5–6, 1974), p. 182.

[10]Fund for the Improvement of Postsecondary Education, *Resources for Change* (Washington, D.C.: U.S. Government Printing Office, 1975), p. 136.

It will be fascinating to see the kinds of "truths in advertising" that emerge from these grants. There is a range of likely outcomes. Institutional information could be developed that exposes both the presumed advantages and the disadvantages of scale. On the other hand, the prospectus might be a more sophisticated, but not necessarily more honest, description of the institution. Students may use the information to make wiser choices about where and whether to enroll; or the prospectus may have no bearing on institutional choice. In the final analysis, it may not matter whether an institution "reveals" itself, since financial pressures frequently dictate the range of choices— little or no money usually means a student is going to a large public state-supported institution.

Nevertheless, students ought to be armed with as much preliminary information as possible to help them get the most from their college experience. The problem with this approach is that it presumes that students must accommodate themselves to the system as it is. But the Fund's not-so-hidden agenda is that by providing an opportunity for an institution to be more fully known, we are aiding institutional reformers to push for needed changes.

The Fund's interest in individualized instruction and consumer education arose, in part, because we were concerned about the relationship of size to educational quality. But these two strategies are proving themselves more useful as responses to the diversity of learners than to the number of learners. We still have not found a way to deal with the problems of size. Administrators and faculty in large institutions have little comprehension of and control over the character and size of colleges and universities. Boards of trustees and state legislatures believe that reducing size automatically means increasing costs. The Fund has given grants to a number of "cluster" colleges at large institutions but it is unclear whether these efforts will survive beyond the expiration of outside funding. Starting costs are naturally high, but it is not necessarily true that once in operation cluster colleges cost more per student than traditional large-scale programs. It is hoped that some will last long enough to prove that they can be economical.

One encouraging sign is that advocates of these new cluster

colleges are beginning to talk about "diseconomies of scale."[11]
These reformers are realizing that they cannot convince administrators of the merits of educating in smaller units without talking about costs. In the past, faculty would gloss over the cost
of new programs and emphasize instead subjective evidence
of student satisfaction to justify their programs. Now, they are
developing ways of comparing "wastefulness" in traditional programs—attrition rates, for example—and comparing these hidden costs with their smaller, more successful efforts.

It is time to expand the dialogue about diseconomies of
scale. Are large, multicampus, multipurpose, comprehensive
institutions really cost effective? Are the figures of the Carnegie
Commission merely useful guidelines or could they be examined
closely to see the cost of traditional notions of cost effectiveness?
Can we afford to be talking about even greater consolidation of
institutions? What will be lost, and what can possibly be gained
from combining the state and city of New York systems to create
a university system of a half million students? The state legislature of Massachusetts has been talking about consolidating the
University of Massachusetts and the Massachusetts State College
system. Although cost saving is a legitimate rationale for such
deliberations, it should not be the only one. The educational
leadership in Massachusetts and throughout the nation should
begin to question what is lost in bigger education.

We are just starting to question whether big is beautiful
in a whole array of human service fields. The names Willow-
brook, Bellevue, and Attica conjure up dehumanizing environments. Will educators be the last to confront our idolatry
of giantism? When does the sheer size of an institution become
counterproductive to learning and personal growth? I am convinced the reason we have not been talking about size and scale
is that we mistakenly assumed that the only way to increase access and commit ourselves to an egalitarian educational system
is to put individuals in larger places. To talk small is not to talk of

[11]For an early discussion of this issue, see V. Smith, "More for Less:
Higher Education's New Priority," in L. Wilson and D. Mills (Eds.), *Universal
Higher Education: Costs and Benefits* (Washington, D.C.: American Council
on Education, 1971): 123–141.

cutbacks or limiting enrollment. Rather, it is to talk about doing a better job of educating people by creating meaningful and manageable learning environments.

In the absence of a definitive study of institutional size in relation to student development, I would like to offer my own "diseconomies-of-scale" scale. Educational institutions are too big when, after one year:

1. Students cannot name and identify seventy-five other students.
2. Faculty cannot name and identify twenty-five students who are not majoring in their department.
3. Faculty cannot name and identify twenty-five faculty in other departments.
4. There is no place on campus that can accommodate all the students affiliated with that educational division.
5. It takes longer than one hour to fill out registration forms.
6. Administrators do not have time to teach a class or serve as academic advisors.
7. The only people the president can identify by name on the student and faculty senates are the two who head those bodies.
8. Administrators cannot name and identify twenty-five faculty members half of whom hold ranks below that of associate professor.
9. A faculty member has to spend a year to get a new course approved on an experimental basis.
10. Graduation has to be held off campus.

Obviously, this list is not definitive. What is important is that it presumes no minimum or maximum figures, although an institution with more than 10,000 students would probably have difficulty fulfilling all points. We need to put a brake on our unquestioning reliance on economies of scale. There is a limit to a person's ability to learn and grow in an environment that makes him or her disappear in a sea of faces or, what is worse yet, become so wrapped up in a solitary learning activity that there is little opportunity to learn with and from others.

Perhaps the poet John Ciardi said it best. In his collection *Person to Person,* there is a poem entitled "The Size of Song":

Some rule of birds kills off the song
in any that begin to grow
much larger than a fist or so.
What happens as they move along
to power and size? Something goes wrong.[12]

---

[12]J. Ciardi, *Person to Person* (New Brunswick, N.J.: Rutgers University Press, 1964), p. 3.

3

Equality, Excellence, and a Missing Link

Benjamin DeMott

The classic positions in the contemporary quality-equality debate are well summarized in two pieces of writing about open admissions at the City University of New York. The first is a 1973 article on the subject by Martin Mayer. The passage I quote comes at the close of a summary of various remediation disasters in the city system classrooms and libraries. It adopts the rhetoric of the curse in discussing the underqualified young people who have been promoted to the status of college student and preprofessional: "a unidimensional measure of academic excellence sets a special, higher floor for many occupations and professions. The ardently egalitarian . . . should cross a river on a bridge designed by an engineer from an engineering school where students were admitted by lottery . . . their injuries should then be treated by a doctor from a medical school where students were admitted by lottery . . . their heirs' malpractice suit should then be tried by a lawyer from a law school where students were admitted by lottery."[1]

The second passage occurs in a defense of open admission by Timothy Healy, vice chancellor of the City University of New York, and reads as follows:

> *There is really no exaggeration in saying that there is nothing in our history, in our literature, in our politics, in our understanding of ourselves, in the hopes and dreams we build for this nation, that the [minority American] does not see and react to differently. . . . It is precisely that difference which is his greatest gift. Through him we can learn to look at ourselves in a new way . . . As long as there is another vision, and we do not incorporate it into our seeing, we are the poorer. . . . To every aspect of our inheritance, we as Americans bring a new perspective—and black Americans will add to it . . . the Greek drama . . . Shakespeare . . . Dylan Thomas or John Donne . . . every artist and philosopher who has worked into words or color or sound his own sense of alienation, or of otherness, or of frustration. How close to Medea's anger, to Caliban's poetry, to Tess's lonely self-evaluation have these young people lived and breathed and suffered. If they had the chance and the training, they might just revitalize the weightiest corpse in the academic morgue, the* litterae humaniores.[2]

The differences between these snippets are obvious: Mayer's literary character, like that of many of his persuasion in the period, is marked by a taunting stiffness, and by a keenness for the example in which mediocrity maims and kills rather than simply muddles along harmlessly in the basement or attic. Healy, like most of *his* persuasion, seems gregarious, generous, a shade unbuttoned, but likeably troubled by the thought that occasionally parties are thrown on this earth to which not all living creatures are invited.

The resemblances matter more than the differences, however. The first resemblance is that both writers avoid the question of how higher education can best serve the interests of a democratic polity. Doubtless both Healy and Mayer would agree, if pressed, that the absolutely critical matter in a democratic polity is the quality of the vote, and that our aim must be

---

[1]M. Mayer, "Higher Education for All? The Case for Open Admissions," *Commentary*, 1973, *55*, 47.

[2]T. Healey, "Will Everyman Destroy the Universe?" *Saturday Review*, 1969, *55*.

the continuous improvement of the quality of the voter—his
and her devotion to freedom, his and her competence to recognize and elect leaders whose concern for the whole life of the
state is intelligently judged and compassionate. But in this out-
ing, as in much of the contemporary equality-excellence debate,
awareness of the national goal seems cramped or partial. The
spokesman for excellence writes as though convinced that the
quality of the vote will take care of itself if the education of
bridge designers, emergency ward interns and liability lawyers
is uncorrupted. The spokesman for equality writes as though
convinced that devotion to freedom will be enhanced if those
hitherto excluded are brought to the campus and allowed to
express opinions in the vicinity of those who have been preparing themselves for years for the study of English composition,
Nietzsche, thermodynamics, and the rest. To repeat: both writers appear to make assumptions about what is educationally
best for the welfare of all, but neither sets those assumptions
under critical scrutiny. And in this respect each stands as a fair
representative of most entrants into this cultural debate.

The second likeness between the two classic passages is
their agreement on the pivotal cultural significance of the academic institution, whether as guardian of unidimensional standards or as potential sponsor of intercultural exchange. Implicit
in the positions of both is a feeling that the teaching and learning responsibilities and aspirations of the society must be left
almost exclusively in the charge of academic institutions; that the
ranking of learning activities (which ones should be esteemed,
that is, and which not esteemed) must also be left in the charge
of academic institutions; that there are few places (or none) to
look, either for the creation of standards or for pointed cultural
exchange, save to the established, university-based academic
disciplines; and that a denial of equal access to higher education—cause for sadness to one writer, pleasure to the other—
means to both men the rejection of equality as a value.

I regard these as disabling convictions—which is to say,
I believe that the larger political context must figure in the
quality-equality debate, and that discussions of access and standards must reflect awareness that the preservation of our political system depends on a vivid consciousness of choice and
a lively devotion to freedom among tens of millions ineligible

for the university. With an apology to those who cannot but see this as a piece of pedantry, I must repeat the pertinent political truisms. Democracy is preoccupied with the task of improving the quality of the vote, and this separates it from the corporate or fascist state that defines people by work function. Democracy is rightly regarded as a teaching and learning society in its marrow, across the board, not merely in its specially labeled "school settings." Levels of "devotion to freedom" will vary in a democratic society with the health of popular belief that participation in teaching and learning, the right of choice in teaching and learning, is sanely, widely distributed. The intelligent voter can be counted on not to confuse the right to participate in the teaching and learning society with the right to enter the graduate professional school of his choice. He or she can also be counted on not to insist that determination of standards of excellence must become the exclusive business of political or nonacademic institutions or that standards created in nonacademic settings must automatically be accorded precedence over university models of excellence. But the intelligent voter will assert that breadth of participation in the teaching and learning society is a pivotal matter in democracy, and that, for this reason standards of excellence in performance other than those developed in and by the university context are at once necessary and salutary.

Unlike the corporate or fascist society, with its rigidly fixed employment identities, democratic society regularly develops standards that supplement and complicate education-based standards. We may take an example from medicine, following Mayer at a distance. In democratic, as in fascist society, all agree that an ill-trained, ill-qualified surgeon is undesirable. The preservation of high professional standards of medical education is crucial to everyone. But the democratic uniqueness lies in a deep, saving *disbelief* that there is one and only one level at which medical education can and should be offered, one and only one level of candidate who can profit from medical education, one and only one way in which the benefits of medical education can be distributed to the public in the form of medical care.

Dozens of American medical schools have experimented successfully with assistant and apprentice doctor programs,

offering two-year training to persons unqualified for regular
medical school training but nevertheless found worthy and
educable, partly on experiential grounds, as assistant doctors.
We know, further, that individual American medical practitioners in Guatemala, Colombia, and elsewhere have developed
the assistant doctor concept, teaching basic diagnostic techniques to intelligent villagers within a radius of a few miles of
the hospital, persons who, using the telephone and other means
of communication, secure assistance and specialized aid from
the hospital-based physician and also treat minor ailments in
the field. We know that in at least one American city, Grand
Rapids, the local medical society and hospital staff (residents and
technicians) have developed a six-month training program for
the city police force, acquainting cops on the beat with techniques
of diagnosis and treatment of emergency medical problems
including cardiac arrest, opening up lines of communication
between individual patrolmen and hospital technicians and
residents, expanding the average patrolman's areas of competence and expertise well beyond that of elementary first aid.
We know that another city—Seattle—has developed a comparable training program for heart disease for its entire adult
citizenry.

What such programs mean, over and above the possibility
that a stroke can be less dangerous on the streets of Grand Rapids or Seattle than on Lake Shore Drive, is that a standard of
performance—of excellence—is brought to birth as a consequence of the contrivance of a new performing situation and a
new performer. When only a single situation is imaginable for
the delivery of medical care (or legal care, or the care of the
English sentence, or the care of persons afflicted with historical
curiosity), the Martin Mayers of this world are correct to seduce
us into terror of the underqualified. But if, as is of course the
case, many situations for the delivery of the various modes of
care are imaginable, then the unidimensional idea of standards
needs revision and the terror needs cooling. As an accident
victim, I should prefer immediate treatment by a trained patrolman on the beat to no treatment at all.

The existence of such programs as those I cite speaks
volumes about the concept of "equality of participation" as distinguished from equality of opportunity or of talent. Hospital

technicians and resident practitioners hitherto closed off from teaching roles—closed off, therefore, from opportunities for sharing their knowledge and experiencing the exhilaration of the teacher-student dynamic—are no longer thus deprived. Peace officers lacking university credentials are permitted, through the program, to participate in modes of learning other than law enforcement. Instruments of this sort are effective means of intensifying belief in equality of participation, nurturing within citizens, on a foundation of truth, not hype, the conviction that the "teaching and learning society" is not primarily a device for insuring that only the rich and their sons and daughters are encouraged to participate in the learning process, but that the teaching and learning society is instead a set of arrangements featuring multiple entry points into the satisfactions of comprehension—and into intuitions of order. Ideally, every profession, every trade in this society, should be engaged in the development of such instruments, and, for many, collaboration with formal institutions of higher learning toward this end is altogether feasible. The overly stark concept of equality in the equality-excellence debate needs the decent clothing provided by the concept of equality of participation. At the same time, the concept of excellence needs to be complicated by awareness of our power to create new excellences, new standards, through new collaborations of persons in work and other settings.

At the level of rhetoric—I do not by any means scorn that level—I tend to be sympathetic with my colleague Henry Steele Commager's assertion that:

> The most promising enterprise in the realm of education would seem to be to make education once again the business of the whole society, to close the gap . . . between school and society; to enlist all available energies of society in the task of Paideia.

> The most practical way to go about this is to create a new network or recreate an old network of educational institutions, "new" only because we have forgotten how old it is; a network of the school and the innumerable voluntary organizations whose functions are educational but whose activities have not for long or ever been educational. We need to construct alliances—when I say "We," I do not mean schools alone but all those interested in education—with the churches, which used to be the major educational institution and were indeed for almost 1500 years.

We need to construct alliances with fraternal orders like the Masons and the Elks and the Woodmen of the World and the Eastern Stars; the great veterans organizations, the American Legion and the VFW; the Boy Scouts and Girl Scouts.

We need to construct alliances with labor unions which have grossly and scandalously neglected their responsibility of an educational character and whom the schools have forgotten or neglected.

We need to construct alliances with the YWCA and the YMCA, the Hadassah, the Knights of Columbus, local Chambers of Commerce, the Bar Associations and other professional organizations . . . all those organizations whose function is not profitmaking but society-making, and whose role should not be limited to the current scene but should be fiduciary. [3]

Scaling these words down to specific proposals for federal intervention, I should recommend that the focus of federal intervention in the immediate future should not be on special educational services to specially designated segments of society. Instead, it should be on those existing programs wherein institutions not engaged in education as conventionally conceived—agencies of government, businesses, unions, youth organizations, arts institutions, and professional associations— have succeeded without federal support in developing lines of communication between themselves and general publics. One might mention—simply for the purpose of citing a few possible growing points—the American Bar Association's Special Committee on Youth Education for Citizenship, which works to further expansion of law-related studies in the lower schools; Action, the National Student Volunteer Program, which encourages volunteer programs in the lower schools through teacher and coordinator training sessions; Executive High School Internships of America, which enrolls two thousand students annually as unpaid special assistants to senior officials or organizations and institutions within local communities; the National Commission on Resources for Youth, which collects and disseminates information on community involvement programs for youth; Students Work with the Handicapped, a California organization sponsoring high school students and college freshmen as resource recreational and instructional

[3] In D. F. Bigelow (Ed.), *School Worlds '76* (Berkeley, Calif.: McCutchan, forthcoming Sept. 1976).

persons for the handicapped and aged; Adopt a Grandparent a similar organization in Connecticut; the Black Liberation School at Ann Arbor, which runs an educational enrichment project using high school students as tutors in nonschool settings; the Children's Art Bazaar Art Gallery in St. Louis, a joint high school student-professional art gallery exhibiting art works from the community; Students Concerned with Public Health, a Philadelphia organization that employs young people to make presentations on public health to elementary school children; and hundreds of other groups and agencies.

The first purpose of this federal intervention should be to foster the kind of mix evident in these already existing, wholly unpretentious initiatives in educational reform—initiatives that link schools and society, youth and grownups, professionals and nonprofessionals, recreating the teaching and learning enterprise as one that engages cross-sections of the powerful and potentially powerful within the society as a whole, and reconceiving standards and evaluation as events occurring not alone in school worlds proper but everywhere in the public air. The greater purpose in expanding the range of settings for participating in teaching and learning is to work toward the creation of new kinds of excellence and new standards, and to open the kind of paths that will show forth the university model as but one route among many toward fulfillment.

By way of personal footnote or digression I might mention that I have known many who press on in their thirties and forties toward the Nirvana of the mid-life doctorate, and while I grant that for some there is point in the undertaking, for others there is largely pathos, vainglory, and misdirection. The assumption that the pursuit of the Ph.D. is a serious, dignified project for anyone, while the projects of the skilled archer, master mechanic, or gifted birdwatcher rank low seems to me absurd. The assimilation of all learning adventure to the norms of the Scholastic Aptitude Test or the specialized contribution to knowledge under the model of nineteenth-century Germanic scholarship has provided this society with one of the thinnest and most juiceless versions of excellence yet known to the West. The creation of the professor as lawgiver, social model, creator of standards stands, by the same token, as one of the most appalling characterological disasters of our time.

Taken in its restricted dimensions, the effort to work toward meanings and dimensions of quality and excellence appropriate to our society could be viewed simply as an attempt to escape the sense of meaninglessness inherent in the cycle of permissiveness and stringency that characterize academic institutions proper. A small liberal arts college I know well now is beginning work on a new curriculum, having abandoned all requirements some years ago. The single injunction from the faculty meeting as guidance was that a required course in science might once again be proposed. In the English department of this college, there are calls for a return to a five-course program for the major—sixteenth-, seventeenth-, eighteenth-, nineteenth-, and twentieth-century literature—pray, naturally, what else? A Return To Standards. The emptiness of such unrationalized change needs no comment.

But there are more exalted dimensions to the effort I have been describing. The swiftest way to suggest them is by pointing out the relationship between the value I describe as "equality of participation" and the older value once summoned by the word "fraternity." The society we would hope for our children is, I believe, a society of collaborative enterprise in which the civilizing force of all modes of learning and teaching is understood, and the distinction of all manner of distinguished performance is perceived and celebrated. It is a society wherein men and women love freedom because the meaning of freedom is made continuously manifest to them as range of choice in learning activities, choice untyrannized by the Great Mother and Father of us all, the University (or the Degree), choice broadened by awareness that multiple entry points to any body of knowledge, at every level of literacy, at virtually every age, can and should be developed. It is a place, this society, wherein the phrase *love of freedom* can be extended without shame or irony to *love of the freedom to know,* and wherein, because of the breadth of participation in learning and teaching, no successful vilification of pointyheads or of "servant classes" is feasible.

I am far from holding that education can save us: indeed, I believe that education locked into the present matrix, however wobbly, of equality and excellence, ranks among the more destructive forces in our midst. We cannot lessen the destructiveness by pretending that salvation requires only that, as penalty for their so-called "lapses" into open admissions and open curricula, and so forth, the sentimentalists transform them-

selves into hardnoses. We should not "despise" equality as a
Red Plot or praise ourselves for having progressed beyond "that
phase." We should instead refocus our thinking about equality
and excellence by introducing the vanished middle link of my
title. I wish to close with two memorable passages from Péguy,
a hero of wisdom. The first passage is a complaint against equality: "The sentiment of equality is not an old sentiment, a per-
petual sentiment, a universal sentiment of first magnitude. At
determined periods it appears in the history of humanity as a
peculiar phenomenon. . . . It often reaches only men loving
the limelight, men loving publicity, and men of government. . . .
Sentiments of equality are artificial sentiments, sentiments obtained by formal construction; bookish, scholastic sentiments."[4]
Then comes the superb celebration of fraternity:

> From age to age, fraternity, whether it puts on the guise of charity
> or the guise of solidarity; whether it is practised towards a guest in the
> name of Zeus Hospitable; whether it welcomes the poor as an image
> of Jesus Christ or whether it establishes a minimum wage for workmen;
> whether it invests the citizen of the world, introducing him by baptism
> into the universal communion; or whether by the improvement of
> economic conditions it introduces him into the international city, this
> fraternity is a living, deeprooted, imperishable human sentiment. It
> is an old sentiment which has been maintained from generation to
> generation, from culture to culture. By far in advance of the civiliza-
> tions of antiquity, it has been maintained in the Christian civilization
> and remains and will doubtless flourish in modern civilization. It is
> one of the best among good sentiments. It is a sentiment at once deeply
> conservative and deeply revolutionary. It is one of the principal among
> the sentiments which have made humanity, which have maintained it,
> which will doubtless free it. It is a great sentiment, one of great moment,
> of great history, of great future. It is a great and noble sentiment, old
> as the world and it has made the world.[5]

When fraternity is allowed its proper role, I should add,
when guilt and sentimentality and sniffishness have been overcome, when fraternity is allowed to remake the structure of
teaching and learning in a democratic society, we shall not have
to frame a choice between equality and excellence. For we shall
have learned how to work simultaneously toward both great
goals.

[4]Péguy, *Basic Verities* (New York, 1943), p. 63.
[5]Péguy, pp. 60–61.

Education and the
Free Self

Stephen K. Bailey

For decades Americans have been experiencing a series of frightening escalations: an escalation of volume in the world of sound; of violence in life, which is reflected (and perhaps fomented) by the mass media; of risk in sports spectaculars; and of hard pornography in books, magazines, and movies. The net result of these neural onslaughts has been not only an increase in violence and crime but also a massive brutalization of our sensibilities. Diversions based solely on "kicks" lead to the demonic and the grotesque and ultimately to a corrosive boredom on the part of those who have seen or heard every-

These remarks are an abridgment of sections of a book, *The Purposes of Education,* published in the summer of 1976 by Phi Delta Kappa.

thing. Estelle R. Ramey has already identified boredom as "the most prevalent American disease."[1]

Television addiction and other passive forms of recreation among the young appear to have other undesirable effects. These passive pursuits have been cited as possible contributors to the startling decrease in both verbal and mathematical skills as measured by the major national testing agencies.[2] Careful students of the influence of television on the American culture are beginning to identify even more unhappy consequences: a shortening of viewers' attention spans; a debasing of social and cultural values, to the extent that sensitivity to even violence and love are narcotized; a propensity to respond to the stimuli of the moment; a false sense of the possibilities of democracy; and a concomitant disenchantment with the political process (heavy television viewers, according to Michael Robinson, are more apt to be turned off by politics than are light viewers).[3] These consequences have implications far beyond the free self, but they also mightily influence the nature and condition of the free self.

Violence, speed, noise, kicks, and other forms and intensities of stimuli might be condoned if they brought a heightened sense of joy or inner satisfaction to most people. But instead they tend to leave people jangled and fretful. They intensify the search for quick fixes to boredom and loneliness and yet end by stimulating both. Surely, the educational system can help people have more creative engagements with the world than are offered by television. For if the free self is appropriately cultivated, its felicitous admixture of playfulness, concentration, and socializing can affect and enrich the worlds of work, day-to-day coping, and citizenship. The life of an individual then becomes not a mere segment of existence but a quality of existence.

[1]E. Ramey, "Boredom: The Most Prevalent American Disease," *Harpers,* Nov. 1974, *248.*

[2]See *College Board Services 1974–1975,* Admissions Testing Program, College Entrance Examination Board, New York, 1975.

[3]See Douglass Cater, *TV and the Thinking Person: A Policy Paper,* the Aspen Institute of Humanistic Studies, Aspen, Colorado, 1975. See also Douglass Cater and Stephen Strickland, *TV Violence and the Child* (New York: Russell Sage, 1975).

The educational system knows far more about the pursuit of happiness than is generally understood. An examination of our human inheritance reveals that lasting inner satisfaction comes from four sources: creating and appreciating beauty, enhancing physical well-being, performing obligations of service, and intensifying intellectual and emotional discovery. Education at its best can lead to each one of these satisfactions.

Education for creating and appreciating beauty, the first source of satisfaction available to the free self, is highly complex.

To begin with, there is an extraordinary range of esthetic preferences. Those who like Raphael rarely like Dali. Mozart lovers often find electronic music baffling. Baroque architecture offends functionalists. Yeats and Pound wrote poetry for different audiences. One high function of education is to enrich esthetic sympathies and tastes. This enrichment may not alter preferences, but it will extend perceptions, human understandings, and rewarding discourse. At the same time, within any particular pattern of esthetic preferences, education can greatly enrich an individual's understanding of the conditions of lasting satisfaction.

If one judges by the historic themes and grace notes of poetry and prose, as well as by contemporary evidence, human beings find enormous esthetic satisfactions in the elemental beauties of nature. Homer's "rosy-fingered dawn," the psalmist who lifted his "eyes unto the hills," Shakespeare's "bank where the wild thyme blows," Wordsworth's "lonely as a cloud," Shelley's "blythe spirit," Yeats's "bee-loud glade," Masefield's "lonely sea and the sky"—these poetic references to nature are familiar to the English-speaking world. Virtually every written and oral language in every epoch and on every inhabited piece of the earth's surface contains expressions of awe, wonder, and delight induced by the beauties of nature. I have been privileged in my work to travel widely. I already knew in exquisite detail what struck the spacemen so vividly from the vantage point of the moon: how incredibly beautiful the world is. I have seen pink on the glaciers of New Zealand's southern Alps; a blood-red sun setting behind the dunes of the Libyan desert; the blue of the midnight moon on the snows of Kilimanjaro; a furtive mist edging the purple wilds of the Scottish moors; a montage of rocks, shells, and sea flowers in the tide pools of County Cork;

the bounding swivel of an African impala; the defiant majesty of the Hindu Kush; Canada geese in all their mottled glory swimming their tidy file through the marshes of Kezar Lake in western Maine.

In each case, esthetic satisfaction was enhanced by solitude or by good companionship. Any number of intrusions or dissonances could have curbed or destroyed the moment: a quarrel, a loud radio, a noisy truck or motor bike, a rifle shot, a pall of factory smoke, a half-dozen discarded beer cans, raucous laughter, a roadside advertisement, the smelly effluent of a paper mill. On the other hand, the beauty could have been enhanced by greater knowledge: historical associations; geological, astronomical, oceanographic, and botanical nomenclature and principles; apt literary and religious allusions from the recesses of memory. I am convinced that dedicated and knowledgable bird-watchers derive far more from forest meanderings than I do. My wife, who is on a first-name basis with trees and flowers, increases the discrimination and the sense of belonging of those who walk or ride with her through natural settings. This is not to say that natural beauty is satisfying only to the learned but rather that the esthetic satisfactions related to natural beauty can be enhanced greatly by education.

What is true of the satisfactions of nature applies equally to satisfaction in the arts. Most people spend their lives oblivious to the intense, lasting satisfactions of artistic expression. Most of us settle for fleeting glimpses of the world of esthetic adventure. We are understandably put off by those who feign knowledge of this treasure-filled landscape in order to bolster their sagging egos or their social status. Again, there is no need to denigrate the untutored delights of commonplace esthetic experiences: a pretty dress, a haunting ballad, a good-looking car, a handsome building, a pleasant flower arrangement, a beautifully furnished room. Nor does it follow that one has not lived unless one really understands chamber music, opera, classical ballet, or abstract art. No devices measure intensities of satisfaction in esthetic tastes and preferences. The classical philosophical conundrum of whether beauty is objective or subjective is still with us, and is unlikely to be resolved. Some art pleases precisely because it rolls over us like a cool wave on a hot beach, because it massages or stimulates noncognitive nerve ends. On the creative side, some art pleases simply because it calls for little effort: barbershop harmonizing, temple rubbings, casual picture taking.

Overall, however, art that leaves a legacy of long-term satisfaction, that holds its power to delight and enrich for generations, is usually the result of great effort. It is the result, literally, of pain: the pain of skill mastery, of discriminating thought, of cultivated subtlety. The fallacy in the esthetics of those who "let it all hang out" is that the exposed flab of such "art" is ugly. Furthermore, extemporaneous, undisciplined expression is, within a short time, colossally boring. An unrehearsed play, an untuned orchestra, a slapdash finger painting, an unedited manuscript, a loose pile of museum artifacts, an unchoreographed ballet—these tend to attract limited interest because mind has not been imposed on emotion, arrangement, or activity. All great art is an extraordinarily intellectual exercise. On the creative side, it is the disciplined manipulation of signals from the unconscious self. On the receiving side, the depth of one's impressions seems to be a direct function of how much one is able to bring, intellectually and emotionally, to the esthetic engagement. It is impossible to derive much satisfaction from watching a Shakespearean play if one is equipped with an English vocabulary of only 1,500 words, just as most of the beauty of an Andrea del Sarto painting would be lost on someone who is color-blind. Ibsen's *Doll's House* has special meaning for those engaged in the struggle for women's liberation. The beauty of the Parthenon grows in the minds of those who have pondered esthetic proportions or studied the culture of fifth century Athens.

How to offer instruction in the arts should be a matter of highest educational priority. We are being all but deadened esthetically by the violence and inanities of most television programing. Too often, education in the arts is considered a frill that can be discarded when budgets are tight. The shortsightedness of this value decision is appalling. If secondary schools disown responsibility in this essential area, then colleges, universities, and community agencies of all kinds must provide corrective and compensating instruction. At the same time, government and voluntary financial support for the Public Broadcasting Service should be increased so that the arts receive more attention on television and radio.

Although the creation and appreciation of beauty is an important frontier in the world of the free self, it is not the only one. The cultivation of bodily skills and fitness (the second source of satisfaction we have mentioned) also can be extraordinarily satisfying. There is a special exhilaration in physical achievements, whether one is balancing a bike, learning to dance, perfecting a second serve, hitting a stick ball, learning to follow through in a golf drive, negotiating a slalom course, or making three out of four free throws in basketball.

One of my favorite people in the world has derived great satisfaction over the years from teaching others how to swim. The development of skill in swimming brings not only grace and stamina but an enormous release from anxiety. Few behavioral changes are more marked or more intrinsically satisfying to both student and instructor than the transformation of an awkward, helpless thrasher into a confident, graceful, versatile swimmer. And swimming opens up a whole range of other aquatic sports—water skiing, sailing, boating, fishing, surfing—that otherwise would likewise be anxiety-ridden.

Many people derive great and lasting satisfactions from preparing and eating good food. If cooking and serving a meal are viewed as creative challenges that bring delight to oneself and to others, the sullenness often associated with kitchen work is transmuted into a happy engagement. Similarly, the cultivation of taste in food and drink can be a rewarding experience and a matter of lifelong satisfaction. Again, these satisfactions take "working at" and can be facilitated by appropriate instruction. Of course, not all the instruction has to take place in formal classrooms: television, radio, tapes, records, informal adult education programs, and self-instruction through reading can all make substantial contributions.

Mastery over the machines and artifacts of technology and over the vagaries of nature is another avenue to satisfaction in the world of the free self. For millions of people, knowledge of "how to make it," "how to fix it," or "how to grow it" is a key to psychic completeness. The process may involve skill with a sewing machine, a mechanical saw, a drill, a hammer, or a cultivator. It may require a knowledge of circuits, solenoids, carburetors, tensile strengths, or fertilizers. It may encompass dexterity with needle and thread, a potter's wheel, a plumber's snake, or a trowel. But once again, "make-it," "fix-it," or "grow-it" skills can be enhanced by formal and informal education.

Patently, not all concern with physical activity needs to be purposive exertion. Lazing or hacking about, watching sports live or on television, laughing at inanities, engaging in festivals, enjoying the company of other people—in measured doses these activities are as important to the free self as a fallow field is to growing crops.

The third major source of satisfactions for the free self is linked with performing obligations of service. It may seem strange to the modern mind to be reminded of concepts like "obligation" and "service," which, however rich their religious and ethical ancestry may be, seem to have lost much of their motive force after the end of the Victorian era. Perhaps their fall from grace was a consequence of the static savagery and unrelieved filth of trench warfare in World War I. Millions of young people on both sides entered that extended conflict with a powerful sense of obligation. Those who survived came out with a shattered idealism.

And yet, even with the twentieth century's massive depreciation of Victorian rhetoric, millions of people have continued to find nourishment in fulfilling perceived obligations and in performing voluntary services. I remember my father donning his greatcoat on a blustery night of snow and wind preparing for a mile walk and saying, "I do not *want* to go to the meeting of the prudential committee of the church, but I *ought* to go!" On returning, he would smile and say simply, "Well, I have done my duty."

Some years ago, during an active political life in Middletown, Connecticut, I came to know hundreds of people who found meaning and satisfaction in performing community services: volunteer firemen, members of library boards, organizers of community chests and United Fund drives, hospital aides, readers for the blind. There is no way of measuring whether this kind of activity is growing or diminishing, but the welfare state, fear of the streets, and the vast amount of time spent watching television have probably eroded the frequency and degree of the service commitment. Nevertheless, a substantial amount of service work is still being done, much of it by young people, and the opportunities for effective service to others are almost limitless. Schools and colleges, churches and synagogues, service clubs and media give attention to identifying service opportunities. What remains to be done—and this could be a function of education—is to emphasize the importance of volunteer service both to the volunteers and to those directly served.

The fourth source of satisfactions is the pleasure of intellectual and emotional discovery. If appropriately exercised, the most durable and satisfying organ of the human body is the brain. Age can cut away at the acuity of memory, but for most people a healthy mind observes with a mixture of anguish and humor the prior deterioration of other parts of the body. Just how the mind functions is still in large measure a mystery. Yet few human experiences can match in sheer exhilaration the rewards of the cultivated human mind at play and at work along the frontiers of its capacity.

Reflecting upon his seven decades of life, E. B. White has said, "I cherish the remembrance of the beauty I have seen. I cherish the grave, compulsive word."[4] That "beauty" and "the grave, compulsive word" should occur in tandem in one of twentieth century America's most truly cultivated minds is surely no accident. The distance between human beings and other primates is most significantly marked by communication. Words are the brain's instruments of internal dialogue, of relating ideas to others, of taming and manipulating objects and events, and of resisting manipulation by others. Words are the rhetorical weapons of peaceful conflict resolution. They are carriers as well as befuddlers of rationality.

Above all, they are the tools of intellectual and emotional discovery. In a world where physical frontiers now need exploration mainly for the purpose of controlling growth and ensuring conservation, and where space frontiers involve high technology and the advanced professional competence of a few, the lasting delights of discovery for most people must be along the frontiers of the mind. For natural scientists, working and playing along this frontier calls for a huge array of the instruments of refined empiricism. For many social scientists and

[4]Interview with E. B. White, *The New York Times,* July 11, 1969, p. 43.

humanists, a knowledge of the modern paraphernalia of symbolic logic (and its limitations) is essential to rewarding discovery. But for most people, intellectual adventure is the experience of crossing clearings made by others, of watching Jacques Cousteau on television or a play of Sophocles on the stage. It is especially the fascination of reading the "grave, compulsive word" wherever it appears in an intellectually challenging and esthetically satisfying way. Reading is essential to most occupations and to most successful coping. It is the key to understanding and improving government. And it is also the most liberating activity that the free self can engage in. The impoverishment of many souls is a direct function of their inability or unwillingness to read.

The rewards of reading are varied. Some reading is largely undemanding and is undertaken for pure relaxation and delight: A. A. Milne, P. G. Wodehouse, Agatha Christie—any reader's list is as good as mine. Here, the rewards of "discovery" come from a felicitous turn of either phrase or events. Some reading is simply a pursuit of knowledge and demands attention on the part of the reader and clarity on the part of the author. Great reading, however, is a search for wisdom through interaction with ideas compellingly expressed. Great reading makes one's own internal dialogue three-dimensional. It creates explosions of insights and sunbursts of esthetic pleasure. It can be suited to mood. Of all human activity, it is the one most congenial to satisfying people's instinct for orientation—their desire to know who they are, where they have come from, their destiny. If the written word contains no final answers, it nevertheless has pointed the way, for it is through reading that generations have shared that psychological nourishment of peace and excitement called *revelation*. What tends to distinguish revelation through reading and revelation through evangelical preaching is that reading permits running and repeated criticism. The mind can tinker with the heart and give it the steadying therapy of continuing reflection.

For those who have never been induced to enter the written world of comparative religion, moral philosophy, cross-cultural literature, or intellectual history, this recitation may seem irrelevant and pretentious. The mood of our present age is both antihistorical and antiprophetic. But as Harvey Cox has pointed out, "Cut a man off from his memories or his visions and he sinks into a depressed state. The same is true for a civilization . . . when a civilization becomes alienated from its past and cynical about its future, as Rome once did, its spiritual energy flags. It stumbles and declines."[5] In a world of future shock and even present shock, the best way to curb alienation and cynicism may be to rediscover the past and to postulate futures that are both reasonable and desirable. Both our past and our future live predominantly and supremely in our universities, our libraries, our arts, and our way of living. Perhaps the most exalted responsibility of education is to guide us to time-tested sources of satisfaction that can help us discover or rediscover who we are and what we have the chance of becoming.

[5]H. Cox, *The Feast of Fools* (New York: Harper & Row, 1971), p. 13.

The Instructional
Revolution

K. Patricia Cross

This bicentennial year marks 200 years of American democracy and, not coincidentally, it marks the end of an era in American higher education. The democratic expansionist era is ending, not so much because of today's declining birthrate, but because higher education, for the first time in its history, is running out of new constituencies to recruit.

The egalitarian ideal has been the principal force behind the growth of higher education for more than a century. Land-grant institutions were created in the last century to accommodate the rising aspirations of the middle class. Community colleges were established in this century to extend college opportunities to still broader segments of the population. Today's nontraditional movement is the last frontier of the expansionist years. It promises to complete the task of making college-level study available to every citizen who wants it.

The pursuit of egalitarian ideals has been responsible for more than growth, however. Directly or indirectly, it has been responsible for most major change in higher education. Each new group of learners absorbed into the colleges has left a permanent imprint on the course of higher education. The land-grant colleges broadened the classical curriculum to include the applied sciences and mechanical arts. They also introduced the massive university campus. The community colleges extended the curriculum still further to include occupational subjects, and they stretched the geographical boundaries of "campus" to include the community. The nontraditional movement is taking the ultimate expansionist step, by promising to use all learning experiences as the curriculum, and to use the world as a campus.

It is now apparent that higher education intends to serve the full spectrum of learners—rich and poor, black and white, male and female, old and young, the able and not-so-able, the mobile and not-so-mobile. It also appears that colleges intend to offer the full range of subject matter—classical, applied, vocational, and avocational. And it is clear that students can be campus residents, commuters, or people who never set foot on a campus.

What does higher education do for an encore in the next century, when, conceptually if not yet practically, it already delivers all of the subjects to all of the people wherever and whenever they want them? What new forces will arise to provide the impetus for change now that there are no new constituencies to recruit? Where will the cutting edge of progress be by the year 2000?

I predict that once we have reached our goal of *education for all*, we will turn our attention to providing *education for each*. Such a goal is infinitely more complex and more demanding than our present goal of providing access for all. We are going to have to be much more thoughtful in the years ahead. The expansionist era of higher education, for all its virtues, has not been especially thoughtful. It has been largely a matter of education by formula—identify a new constituency, find out what it wants and needs, and expand the system to include it.

So far, access is what the new constituencies have wanted and needed most. Low-income students need financial aid; low achievers need open admissions colleges; adults need flexible scheduling; women need access to graduate and professional programs. As we check off the now-familiar needs that the nation has tried to meet, it is clear that these are administrative rather than instructional matters. Administrators on campuses and in state and federal agencies have made major changes in almost every facet of their operations. Financial aid, for example, has increased 6,000 percent since 1954, and awards, once based on scholarly accomplishments, are now computed on economic need. Admissions offices, which once operated to screen people out, now scramble to pull people in.

But the expansionist years have had relatively little effect on the practices of the average faculty member. Most teachers wait patiently for the machinery to move each new wave of students into their relatively unchanging classrooms. As a recent Carnegie report notes, college instruction remains pretty much as it was 300 years ago.[1] Unless learning experiences are redesigned to meet the needs of the new clientele and the changing times, access to college is a hollow victory. The impetus for change in the remaining years of this century will come from a recognition that higher education does not offer all of its constituencies equally good learning experiences.

But instructional change is on the way. Today's timid beginners will accelerate as we move toward the close of this century. By the year 2000, an instructional revolution will have changed higher education in fundamental ways. Signs of that revolution have already appeared. Faculty development is the hottest topic in higher education today, attracting overflow crowds to conferences and workshops. Offices for the improvement of instruction are proliferating like mushrooms after a spring rain. Pedagogical alternatives have also spread rapidly. The use of self-pacing methods in community colleges more than doubled between 1970 and 1974, and Keller Plan courses have swept through university classes in the sciences and social sciences with unprecedented speed.[2]

I count four major pressures for these instructional reforms in higher education. The first and most obvious is the ar-

[1]S. C. Wren, *The College Student and Higher Education Policy* (New York: The Carnegie Foundation for the Advancement of Teaching, 1975).

[2]K. P. Cross, *Accent on Learning: Improving Instruction and Reshaping the Curriculum* (San Francisco: Jossey-Bass, 1976).

rival of the no-growth era. For colleges, this steady state means that improvements of programs and professors must take the form of remodeling rather than of additions. For professors, the arrival of the steady state means the loss of professional mobility and the probable return of loyalty to local institutions. Good teaching may pay off since it is a locally visible activity that contrasts sharply with the nationally recognized research and publication route that upwardly mobile professors have chosen in the past.

The second pressure for the improvement of instruction comes from society's loss of faith in its institutions. Church, state, and school have all suffered a loss in prestige. Taxpayers are demanding accountability, and students are beginning to see themselves as consumers of education. They expect delivery on the promises made in college catalogues. One distressing finding of educational research is that the intellectual and cultural interests of the senior class are more closely related to the interests of the freshman class four years earlier than to anything that happened during their four years in college. The new consumers want something more substantial than club membership for their time and money.

The third pressure for reform results from increased access to higher education. The college degree has lost that part of its glitter that was due to its exclusiveness. As the credential loses value, the competency of the graduates becomes increasingly important. If colleges cannot *select* the qualities they would like to see in their graduating classes, then they had better bend their efforts to *instill* those qualities.

Finally, I think that "New Students," the designation that I reserve for low academic achievers entering open admissions colleges, have done a great deal to force the instructional revolution. Without knowing it, students with poor academic backgrounds have challenged college instructors to look at their ability to teach. Traditional college students who are selected for their motivation and academic skills are no challenge to pedagogy. Given a little direction in the form of assignments and modest incentives in the form of grades, they almost teach themselves. But community college teachers who met the first wave of New Students were first distressed and then challenged when they discovered that the traditional, information-saturated lecture was falling on deaf ears. (It probably falls on the deaf ears of traditional students too, but their study outside of class masks the ineffectiveness of the classroom.) In any event, some of the most exciting instructional reforms are taking place in colleges where New Students are heavily represented. Necessity is the mother of invention.

This introduction leads me to some observations about the reactions of colleges in general to the emerging instructional revolution. At the leading edge the response is energetic, sincere, and full of vitality. In the dragging middle, the response varies from sluggish to recalcitrant. The middle is dragging largely because the average discipline-oriented professor lacks knowledge of the teaching-learning process. It has been said before, and it will probably be reiterated for the next decade, that no professionals have less training for their jobs than college teachers. But it is hard to understand why academicians, who value knowledge, take such perverse pride in maintaining their ignorance about the process of teaching and learning.

There are differences of opinion about how to remedy such ignorance because it is not recognized by many university professors. Most faculty development offices take a low-profile, counseling-bureau approach, offering various services but waiting for faculty to come to them for assistance. James Popham of the University of California at Los Angeles, however, shows impatience with this timorous approach to improving instruction. He writes that

the quality of instruction at the university level is infinitely more inept than most people realize. . . . [but] We would not dream of insulting our professional colleagues by describing [instructional development programs] as "inservice education," even though almost all of them failed to experience anything resembling "preservice education." No, we must gentle up to the college professors with seductively labeled schemes which will entice them to improve, ever so incrementally, their instructional endeavors. . . . While the current efforts to improve university teaching should be applauded, let's make it clear that such applause should be mild.[3]

[3]W. J. Popham, "Higher Education's Commitment to Instructional Development Programs," in D. W. Allen, M. A. Melnik, and C. C. Peele (Eds.), *Reform, Renewal, Reward* (Amherst, Mass.: Clinic to Improve University Teaching, University of Massachusetts, 1975).

It is hard to know what to do for more vigorous applause. One common practice that we should not perpetuate is pretending that years of experience or even scholarly reputation are necessarily related to the quality of undergraduate instruction. As college professors are quick to point out in these days of enthusiasm for experiential learning, experience alone does not constitute knowledge. Yet too many faculty workshops attempt to legitimize themselves by opening with an address by a respected scholar who knows a lot about his discipline but very little about the learning process. After listening to one such speaker at a workshop on instructional improvement, I drafted some remarks for the unlikely day when the educator might be invited to address a meeting of scientists on their specialty. First, the distinguished scholar addressing the faculty development workshop:

I have never had a course on teaching, and I know nothing of the various theories of learning. I have, however, taught in a college classroom for twenty-five years. While I am not familiar with so-called teaching methods and techniques, I hope that my experience and observations will be helpful and useful to other teachers.

There is, of course, no real science of education in the sense that experts can predict with certainty who will succeed in college. Nor do we know how to create the most desirable learning conditions. Therefore, it seems to me that I, who am in the classroom every day, can probably be as helpful in understanding learning as can researchers who rarely teach in the reality of the classroom.

While I admit that there are some techniques that can probably be used to improve the performance of the average *teacher—instructional objectives and faculty evaluation perhaps—the master teacher is not dependent on tools and techniques. He has a sensitivity for learning—a feel for when real learning is taking place. A teacher who loves his subject and who personally experiences the joy of learning is probably in the best position to create such satisfactions for others.*

Now let us parallel this real-life story with the unlikely scenario in which a distinguished educator is invited to address a group of scientists—in this case meteorologists—who are eager to lend credibility to their work because their weather predictions have been criticized recently. In this fantasy, there is the familiar exploitation of the professor's distinction and the unrealistic hope that his personal experience with weather conditions will contribute important insights to their workshop on meteorology. His remarks might go like this:

I have never studied meteorology, and I know nothing of the various theories on the subject. I have, however, lived in the physical world for forty-five years. While I have no idea what causes certain weather patterns or how to induce rain when we need it, I do put on the snow tires in winter and carry an umbrella when it rains. I hope my experience and observations will be helpful and useful to professional meteorologists.

There is, of course, no real science of weather in the sense that experts can predict with certainty whether it will rain on a given day. Nor do we know how to bring about the most desirable weather conditions. Therefore, it seems to me that I, who live with the weather every day, can probably be as helpful in understanding it as can researchers who rarely venture into the reality of a rainstorm or a blizzard.

While I admit that there are some techniques that can probably be used to improve the performance of the average meteorologist—barometers and weather maps, perhaps—the master meteorologist is not dependent on tools and techniques; he has a sensitivity to the weather, and perhaps a good arthritic knee. A meteorologist who loves weather and who personally experiences the joys of beautiful days is probably in the best position to create such satisfactions for others.

My analogy between the science of meteorology and the science of teaching was carefully chosen. Neither science is infallible. Both are better at predicting than at creating desirable climates for growth. Nevertheless, the weather bureau has a better understanding of climatic conditions than some farmers would like to admit, and educators and psychologists know much more about learning than some professors would like to admit.

Another hurdle that must be cleared in order to improve instruction is the academic distrust of experimentation and innovation. It is hard to explain why college professors, who are so curious and experimental with respect to the subject matter of their own disciplines, should be so conservative about teaching. I recently spoke with a college dean who stated emphatically that the first priority of colleges should be the improvement of traditional instruction, and only when that was perfected should colleges spend money to support innovation. In the midst of being grateful for his support of the idea that traditional instruction could be improved, I asked myself where General Electric would be if they had decided to perfect the ice box before starting to work on the refrigerator. Fortunately, some people have started work on the instructional equivalents of refrigerators, and the consumer who has experienced even a primitive version of the refrigerator may come to demand it over some pretty high-quality ice boxes. Many consumers of new teaching-learning strategies are now in community colleges. Today, a really good community college offers a wide array of teaching-learning alternatives, such as open-date enrollment in self-paced courses, hands-on learning experiences in well-equipped laboratories, the latest in computer-assisted and computer-managed instruction, learning laboratories open round the clock and staffed by dedicated learning specialists, and teachers who want to be teachers rather than researchers. When these consumers, used to the joys and conveniences of the refrigerator, graduate to a four-year institution offering a good ice box for a lot more money, we may see a student rebellion that will surpass that of the 1960s in its impact on education. This rebellion can be avoided if teaching innovators can blaze a trail that looks promising enough for the dragging middle to follow. And I think that is happening. Let me give some examples.

First, we are beginning to apply what we know about the teaching-learning process to college teaching. One of the pioneers of the instructional revolution is Fred Keller, a psychologist who simply applied what he had been teaching about learning to the design of his own classes. The Keller Plan, also known as the Personalized System of Instruction or PSI, has spread rapidly throughout the social and physical sciences. The learning principles incorporated into PSI are simple: the learning tasks must be clearly defined; students must respond actively; immediate rewards must be granted for appropriate responses; and foundation units must be learned thoroughly before advanced units are attempted.

The research evaluations that have been part of the PSI movement from the beginning indicate that it does what it purports to do very well. PSI students retain their learning longer, they do better in subsequent courses, and an impressive majority give their PSI courses higher ratings than they give lecture courses in the same subjects.[4] PSI is not a panacea, but, as one example of successfully applied learning theory, it demonstrates the potential of the instructional revolution.

A second sign of the instructional revolution is the recognition of the strengths and weaknesses of teaching alternatives. A teaching method need not be new or innovative to be effective, but it must be used for what it can accomplish. Lectures are used poorly when they present information easily available through the more carefully worded, self-paced medium of a good textbook. Lectures are used well when they are planned to present new ideas, to inspire, or to illustrate the process of a scholarly mind at work. Because few classroom lectures are prepared with such care, we might do better to videotape outstanding lectures with all of the quality control that technology offers. Take another example. Discussions are a waste of everyone's time when they consist of instructor questions and student recitations of content that might be handled better through computer-assisted instruction, which gives the student maximum feedback in minimum time without wasting the time of other students. Discussions are useful when they challenge students to formulate, communicate, and react to ideas. But how often are class discussions used to stimulate active thinking, and how rigorous are they in demanding clear articulation?

Examples of the appropriate uses of alternative teaching strategies could be extended. The audiotutorial methods of Sam Postlethwait at Purdue University exemplify a carefully planned learning system. With the use of an audio cassette, the instructor can arrange laboratory experiences so they occur in the most meaningful sequence. Students no longer need to read the text, hear the lecture, and then do the experiment. They may read a portion of the text while handling physical specimens in their laboratory carrel. They may view a filmed demonstration while they are conducting their own experiment, and they may test their understanding in quiz sessions with other students.

The humanities seem to be having some trouble launching an instructional revolution in this behaviorist era of instructional improvement. However, television, film, and other

[4] J. A. Kulik and C. L. C. Kulik, "Effectiveness of the Personalized System of Instruction," *Engineering Education* 66 (December 1975): 228–231.

methods for utilizing a wider range of sensory channels in learning are having cultural impact. Television programs such as
The Ascent of Man and *The Adams Chronicles* represent an important direction of instructional change. The new adult market
offers an especially attractive challenge to the humanities, but
instruction will have to be good to attract and hold noncaptive,
unsubsidized adult learners.

A third necessary step in the instructional revolution is
the development of more discriminating consumers of education. If lifelong learning lies in the futures of our students, then
we need to provide them with the consumer skills to make wise
choices among many learning alternatives. As the instructional
revolution develops, students will be exposed to a wide array
of learning experiences and will be able to do some comparative
shopping. But students should learn something about their own
cognitive styles and about human learning in general. An excellent lecture course may be a good investment for some students, but it might be a poor investment for others who need
to learn basic skills or who need practice in formulating and
articulating ideas. In the long run, sophisticated consumer-
students will probably do more to challenge faculty performance
than any incentive system we could devise. Most people do their
best when they know that they have a discriminating audience.
Just as a chef will outdo himself for a table of gourmet diners, so
a faculty member is likely to rise to the challenge of discriminating learners. But students are not critical consumers at present.
Many are content with the ice box because they do not know
that the refrigerator exists. And students are notoriously chari-
table in rating their instructors. Unlike some of their professors,
they seem to feel no obligation to preserve standards by rating
on the curve. Some faculty are lulled into a false sense of secu-
rity by their gratifyingly high student ratings. Faculty at one
typical institution, for example, averaged 5.5 on a 7-point scale,[5]
and the overwhelming majority of teachers at almost any institution are rated above the average point on the scale. Personally,
I doubt that there is any cause-and-effect relationship between

[5]M. Hildebrand, "How to Recommend Promotion for a Mediocre
Teacher Without Actually Lying," *Journal of Higher Education 43* (1972):
44–62.

inflated student grades and inflated faculty ratings as some observers have charged. Rather, I think that no one, student or teacher, knows how good teaching could be.

By and large, college faculty are dedicated, conscientious professionals. Good teaching is not so much a question of urging professors to work harder as of getting them to acknowledge that they are not practicing their profession very skillfully. Most university administrations assume they will improve teaching by tying salary and promotion to valid evaluations of teaching effectiveness. Perhaps so, but our preliminary interviews with faculty members at the University of Nebraska indicate that the greatest reward that can be offered for good teaching is the self-satisfaction that comes from doing a good job and seeing students develop into thinking individuals. This is not to say that we can afford to let distinguished teachers play second fiddle to distinguished researchers in matters of promotion and pay, but it is to admit that there are many ways to improve teaching besides expensive monetary incentive systems.

The fourth step in the instructional revolution lies a few years in the future, but it is as essential to the improvement of learning as anything I have mentioned. I believe that before the end of this century we will see dramatic changes in the structure and organization of instructional programs. Specifically, we will have to take a hard look at the three sacred cows of education: the semester, the credit hour, and the grading system.

These sacred cows are our measures of learning, and they are woefully inadequate. The semester represents mass education at its worst. Under the bind of the semester, we batch people of vastly different backgrounds and abilities and do what we can for them in the time available. It is as though the Ford assembly line batched cars that were almost completed with cars that were barely started, and did what they could for each car in the time available at each station. Imagine conscientious workers, comparable to a faculty, working hard to get the first wheel on some cars and the last wheel on others. Predictably, at the end of the line, there would be cars unable to run because they have only one wheel, cars lurching on three wheels, and cars gliding smoothly on all four wheels. Noting these obvious differences, Ford might compound their original error by grading within batches. The car with three wheels will rate an A if it appears in a batch lacking four-wheeled cars, but it will receive a B if it passes through the line with some four-wheeled cars. Quality control may note with some dismay that the average Ford car has only two wheels, but management will point out that after all each car has been through the standard eight stations, and by definition, eight stations equals one car, much as eight semesters equals one degree.

The assembly line that we have tried to apply to education does not work when the incoming units vary as much as they do in higher education. Education, if it is to be useful to the majority, will have to abandon the assembly-line approach, in favor of customized or individualized education. The simple fact is that the existence of individual differences in learning rates precludes the efficiency of the assembly line. The semester makes no sense if students are encouraged to learn at their own pace. Grades make no sense in self-paced or individualized learning because there is no cut-off time, such as the end of a semester, when decisions are made about how much the student learned relative to his peers. In individualized learning, the cut-off point occurs when the student has learned the material to a set criterion level. If comparative grades at the end of a standard semester become useless as measures of learning, then the replacement is likely to be variable or modular credit in which students collect educational credits for what they know.

Many people reject individualized education for financial rather than pedagogical reasons. How is it that so few quarrel with the fact that traditional education is extravagantly individualized for teachers? Each teacher is permitted to design a unique course that capitalizes on his or her knowledge, abilities, and interests. Students are then expected to adjust their learning paces and abilities to suit the teacher. The tradition of individualization for the faculty is deeply ingrained. But it seems inconsistent to support the design of literally thousands of separate courses on roughly the same subject while questioning the expense of helping students learn what has been so extravagantly prepared. I am not advocating a national curriculum— far from it. I am suggesting that teachers at the undergraduate level, especially the first two years, can get as much satisfaction from the challenge of helping individuals learn as they can from designing a course in the image of their graduate training.

British Open University has demonstrated the feasibility of high quality, centrally produced courses, and Empire State College and other nontraditional institutions in this country have demonstrated the effectiveness of individualized learning contracts. Keller Plan courses have demonstrated the effectiveness of self-paced methods. A judicious use of combinations and alternatives appears to make good fiscal and pedagogical sense.

The challenge now facing higher education is to provide the best education possible for each individual learner. We were pushed into this instructional revolution by such external factors as the steady state, consumer demands for accountability, and the egalitarian challenge of open admissions. In response to the push that turned to shove, there has developed a leading edge of instructional reform that is blazing promising new paths. The new pedagogies of individualized instruction are making great strides both in their acceptability to professors and in their accountability in research evaluations. Staff development programs are making some progress in helping college teachers recognize the strengths and limitations of a broadening array of teaching strategies. As the instructional revolution opens new experiences and new choices, students will become increasingly sophisticated consumers of their own education. By the turn of the century, the instructional revolution may well have produced a fundamental reform of the structures and measures of higher education.

6

Faculty Development: The State of the Art

Jerry G. Gaff

Development has rapidly become a national pastime in higher education. Programs are established to implement it, grants are given to support it, workshops and conferences are arranged to examine it, and journals are determined to spread it. There are programs concerned with the development of department chairpersons, deans, nonacademic staff, presidents, and trustees; there are even programs to develop developers of these various groups. But by far the largest part of the current development movement is concerned with faculty development—the improvement of teachers and teaching.

Most faculty development programs rest on several explicit or implicit assumptions. The first is that faculty members are the most important educational resource of a college or university, and that special care must be taken to preserve and extend their talents and thereby enhance their value. A second assumption is that teaching is the primary, though by no means only, professional activity of most faculty members, and most want to excell as teachers. Third, because most faculty members received no preparation as teachers during their graduate training, they can profit from participation in campus-based programs that help them grow in various aspects of teaching. Another assumption is that each institution and each administrative unit within the institution ought to have a program to develop the talents, interests, and competencies of the professional people it employs. This program needs to be more than a paper plan; it needs to be supported by an appropriate organization, adequate budget, and professional staff. Finally, despite the proliferation of new programs and their uneven quality, the current interest in faculty development is regarded as a long overdue response to a fundamental problem in higher education and is not simply a fad, of which higher education seems to have more than its share.

How does an institution proceed from these assumptions to a development program that will help faculty in their teaching roles? Three approaches are common. Some institutions favor programs that focus on *faculty members* themselves. These programs seek to help faculty acquire more knowledge about teaching and learning issues, learn about alternative approaches or methods of teaching, obtain feedback on their teaching styles from students or colleagues, acquire new skills or techniques, and clarify attitudes and values. A second approach is to focus not on the faculty members but on the *courses* they teach. Programs of this type help faculty members set behavioral objectives for students in various courses, design effective learning experiences for students using media, technology, or other methods, and devise fair and accurate evaluations of student accomplishment. The third approach focuses on the *environment* within which teaching and learning occur. It involves establishing personnel policies that support effective teaching and the development of faculty members, helping department chairpersons and central administrators support the efforts of faculty, and creating a climate of vitality, trust, and openness among colleagues and between faculty and students. These three approaches overlap in many instances and are expressed differently in different institutions. But they are the major forms that current faculty development efforts take.

Before an institution establishes any kind of program, however, it has to come to grips with the question, "Faculty development for what?" The question necessarily involves educational philosophy, and as might be expected, very different answers are given. Some people assume that stimulating and furthering the growth of faculty members is an end in itself, while others see faculty development as a means to improve the education of students or to strengthen the institution. Some seek, through faculty development, to preserve high standards and promote the advancement of knowledge, which they see threatened by a persistent antiintellectualism in America and by increasingly tight external controls over academic programs and budgets. Others see in faculty development an opportunity to redirect the profession toward more egalitarian concerns or a chance to move the professors away from a preoccupation with esoteric specialized knowledge toward more holistic and generally useful knowledge. Some believe the improvement of teaching in traditional contexts should be stressed while others believe the emphasis should be on new roles for faculty and innovative settings. For those who believe that effective teaching engages the whole personality, faculty development is related to personal and career development. On the other hand, those who see teaching as largely a cognitive activity of transfering information and ideas from one mind to another believe faculty development should emphasize classroom techniques and skills. Although this wide range of interpretations makes faculty development ideal for mobilizing diverse interests and establishing programs, it can become a serious hazard in carrying out a program. At the operational stage, more agreement is needed.

Such agreement is not likely to occur unless faculty development is understood as involving matters that transcend any single individual and that affect the entire institution. For instance, members of a committee on which I served to plan a conference on teaching spent some time at the outset discussing their own concerns. Some members were concerned about the larger number of lower-ability students they were finding in their courses. "How do you teach students who don't know how to think?" was the way one person put it. Many were concerned about the situation facing faculty members, including the grim job market, a general demoralization, and the tendency toward privatism. One person remarked, "About one third of the faculty at my place are actively retired." Some members of the committee noted the increasing vocationalist trend and wondered about the future of the liberal arts. Others complained about bureaucracy, and one confessed, "Frankly, I don't have much faith in the possibility of institutional change." Every one of these concerns reflects important basic changes that are taking place in colleges and universities as well as in the larger society. None of these matters can be adequately addressed simply by working with solitary individuals. Faculty development, if done properly, involves institutional development.

Furthermore, the kind of development program that a school chooses ought to be related to the mission, tradition, and distinctive character of the institution. The classical academic hierarchy, in which each institution seeks to be as much like Harvard as possible, is at last giving way to the realization that there are many valuable institutional roles. It is no longer possible, if indeed it ever was, for an institution to be all things to all people. There are simply too many purposes and activities that might legitimately be a part of a college or university. It is becoming increasingly necessary for an institution to choose deliberately which areas of excellence it will pursue. Getting faculty, administration, board, and in many cases the legislature to reach a consensus on this is no easy task—but the alternative is establishing just another program that adds to the cross-purposes of the institution.

Once an institution comes to some understanding about its distinctive character, it can begin to tailor a program to its particular needs. At this point—the implementation stage—several facts should be kept in mind. First, every institution contains a great diversity of faculty members, and a faculty development program ought to provide different kinds of assistance to each. For example, one institution with which I am familiar started as a normal school and hired a faculty to teach teachers. In the late 1950s the school added a liberal arts program and recruited a group of faculty members who had different and broader interests than their predecessors. Then during the 1960s the school grew into a university and recruited a large contingent of Ph.D. scholars. Compared to the first two groups, these young faculty were more interested in research, in working with their academic specializations, rather than in providing a broad general education, and in teaching bright, motivated students rather than in teaching the less able students who increasingly populated the school. Each group felt threatened and frustrated to some extent by the very existence of the others. Not only was there a need to help these various cohort groups live and work productively together, but each group also needed different kinds of support in order to carry out an institutional mission that neither had been hired to serve.

A second point to keep in mind is that a "home-grown" faculty development program is likely to be more durable than one imported from another place. In a fundamental sense, each college or university is a repository of the accumulated knowledge and experience of civilization. Individuals often do not even know that there are others on the campus who are interested in the same things they are or who can help them with their concerns. It should be possible for an institution to function as a talent pool, each faculty member and administrator contributing to others and each free to ask his or her colleagues for assistance. One of the tragedies of the academic profession is that faculty so seldom take advantage of the rich resources of their own institutions to further their understanding and purposes. A sound faculty development program ought to identify the prevailing needs and resources and match them for the benefit of all individuals.

The use of outsiders should also be considered at the implementation stage. Outsiders may be helpful in overcoming obstacles to productive working relationships and setting a new dynamic in motion. At one large institution I visited recently, the vice president for academic affairs told me, "Jerry, we have been emphasizing research here, and now we need to place more emphasis on teaching. But we must go slow and make sure that we have grass roots support among the faculty, because they are strong on research." I left his office to meet with a faculty committee where I was told, "We are interested in some kind of teaching improvement program, but our administration just doesn't value teaching." Then I had the good fortune of having lunch with both, and was able to introduce the two points of view to each other. Frequently, it takes an outsider to establish communication among individuals on the campus, to get people to realize that they share common interests, and to help them start working together. But ultimately communication and cooperation need to be generated and sustained by individuals at the school.

A further principle is that effective faculty development must be an integral part of life on the campus. Some of the most well-known instructional resource centers are located at major universities; they have formal organizations, comparatively large budgets, and highly professional staffs. Despite the visibility of these organizations and scholars, they may not have much impact at their institutions unless they are tied into the campus culture. After speaking at a recent conference I was asked by a professor, "What can you suggest that we do in our own units to improve teaching?" I suggested that he might get a small group of like-minded colleagues together to explore their common interests and that the department might devote a faculty meeting to substantive educational matters rather than to the usual departmental business. He replied that he was the chairman of a department of eighty-five, they had only one meeting per year, and he could not recall the last time a group had talked about pedagogical matters. I have since puzzled about what went on in that *one* meeting. Why would a department bother to have *one* meeting? Be that as it may, I subsequently learned that he was from a Big Ten university that had one of the largest and best known instructional improvement centers in the country—which he had never thought of using. A few years ago, as student protests were sweeping Berkeley, Columbia, Harvard, and Chicago, Burton Clark wrote, "If we did not know it before, we know it now—good scholars and good students can make a bad educational system. Everything depends on how they are put together."[1] The same applies to faculty development. Good people, good organizations, and good reputations do not necessarily make good programs. Everything depends on the way they are put together and how they mesh with the ongoing life of the institution.

By and large, institutions get the kind of faculty development programs they deserve. The institution that is really not

[1] B. R. Clark, "The New University," *American Behavioral Scientist* (May-June 1968): 5.

committed to excellence in undergraduate education may find it stylish to have a teaching improvement unit, but it will be little more than a showcase. The institution that operates in reckless disregard of faculty interests, that does not seek out faculty views in shaping institutional policies, and that makes arbitrary personnel decisions will not be able to convince its faculty that it has their best interests at heart. And the institution that is so concerned about accountability that it fails to provide an adequate budget for faculty development may have a program that is a model of efficiency but that will have little impact. In short, the institution that wants an effective faculty development program ought to first make sure that it believes in people—faculty, students, and administrators—in all their diversity and complexity. It should then incorporate that belief in all of its operating policies and practices.

Finally, if faculty development is to be more than a passing fad, it needs to become an established part of institutional organization. Institutionalizing programs so that they enter the mainstream of academic life will require work on several fronts. Most current programs involve modest numbers of faculty members who participate voluntarily as an "overload" and who receive little or no recognition for their efforts. More faculty need to become involved. Self-development should become part of one's professional obligation. It should become a regular part of the workload, and faculty should get rewarded for their efforts. Budgets, which are typically meager and frequently contain short-term grant money, need to be increased and stabilized. Too many programs operate as short-term projects with only one or two persons to keep them going. Finally, a lot more evidence of the consequences of faculty development, intended and unintended, is needed. Currently there are descriptions of activities, numbers of participants, and interesting anecdotes, but sound evidence of the impact of professional development programs on participants, on students, and on institutions is very limited.

But what remains to be done is not so awe-inspiring when one considers how much has been accomplished in the few short years since faculty development burst on the scene. Different kinds of programs have been conceived by many different institutions; organizational structures have been built; resources have been obtained and allocated; staff have been recruited and trained; faculty have become involved; and much valuable experience has been gained in this new and promising enterprise. If our future efforts are as successful as our past efforts, teaching will become not just an honorable but also an honored profession.

7

Faculty Evaluation for Accountability

H. Bradley Sagen

Sizable segments of the public, particularly of its elected representatives, suspect that colleges and universities do not contribute effectively to the goals for which public and private funds have been allocated. Because of the labor-intensive nature of higher education, the autonomy granted faculty, and the vagueness of evaluation procedures, such suspicion has often focused on the accountability of individual faculty members. Unless colleges and universities develop more effective programs to evaluate both programs and individuals, public concern will lead to further external control and to decreased resources.

To be accountable, faculty evaluation must achieve a reasonable balance between the position that faculty performance should be judged by professional peers and the position that any profession must be accountable to the society it serves. Achieving this balance will depend on how effectively three basic principles of accountability are carried out. The first of these principles holds that institutions are accountable for achieving goals set by society but that, as professional organizations, they must have autonomy in organizing their activities to pursue these goals. The second principle contends that complex institutions can attain goals most effectively by delegating responsibility to appropriate organizational units. The third principle, which is a logical deduction from the first two, is that individual faculty should be appraised primarily according to their contribution to the unit.

Viewed in this way, faculty evaluation is an integral part of institutional and program evaluation. Such terms as *effective teaching* and *productive scholarship* thus acquire a more precise meaning because they relate to the educational mission of specific programs. Thus, effective teaching may mean one thing in freshman studies and another in advanced professional programs. Failure to establish clear goals and to articulate them in a format that permits evaluation is perhaps the major cause of conflict between educational institutions and society, and between institutions and individual faculty.

At many institutions, faculty evaluation is conducted by peer groups who cannot be held accountable for the consequences of decisions as they affect the welfare of the institution, and who therefore appraise in terms of personal rather than institutional criteria. Conversely, evaluations and personnel decisions at some institutions have become overly centralized and judgments are made by groups or individuals too far removed from the complexity of the individual faculty member's situation. The task is to establish a level of centralization in faculty personnel decisions that permits appropriate peer review yet focuses on institutional goals because the unit itself is accountable. The best size range for a unit responsible for both faculty and program evaluation appears to be about thirty-five to seventy-five faculty members. In small colleges, faculty evaluation can be handled best at the institutional level; in institutions of moderate size, by colleges or divisions; and in the larger universities, by departments or program units.

Faculty can also be evaluated by separate groups for different functions. For example, effectiveness in undergraduate instruction might initially be reviewed by a group composed of those faculty members teaching basic undergraduate courses in several fields, whereas research productivity might be appraised by departmental colleagues pursuing investigations quite similar to those of the person being evaluated.

Faculty evaluation must be concerned not only with the competence of an individual within a position but also with the long-term contribution of that position to the institution. Small departments and other units are generally inappropriate for conducting such evaluation, not only because they emphasize narrow and sometimes irrelevant criteria, but also because small units find it more difficult to adjust resources in the face of changing demands. Delegating responsibility to larger, more comprehensive units permits faculty in some instances to be moved to other tasks as new opportunities emerge.

Emphasizing the professional and institutional nature of faculty evaluation also helps clarify the role of students in evaluation. Evaluative information from students is generally useful and students often function effectively as members of initial review groups. But students cannot be held accountable for their judgments. Nor do their aims always coincide with the aims of the institution or unit. For these reasons, personnel decisions should be made by those professionals accountable for unit performance.

A second criterion of faculty evaluation, justice, both extends and modifies the criterion of organizational effectiveness. Justice in faculty evaluation means two things: due process to protect individual rights, and fairness in the distribution of benefits and burdens.

Due process is well established for cases involving the dismissal of tenured faculty. Its application in such cases has been upheld consistently by the courts. In cases involving the termination of nontenured faculty and in the ongoing evaluation of all faculty, however, due process has been largely a matter of institutional or subunit preference.

Due process in faculty evaluation suffers from two major defects: limitations in the evaluation techniques currently available, and inadequacies in decision-making procedures. Decades of research have failed to produce a satisfactory definition of instructional effectiveness. Even the criterion of student learning is generally unsatisfactory because of disagreements over instructional goals, difficulties in assessing complex changes in behavior, and the yet unsolved problem of determining what contribution an instructor makes to academic learning. Most evaluations of instruction thus rely on process types of assessment. Student ratings appear relatively free from the most obvious sources of bias,[1] but the questions of what features of instruction are actually assessed by such ratings and of the relationship between ratings and student learning have not been answered adequately. Other measures, such as class visitations and colleague ratings, generally lack reliability[2] and contain the possibility of rater bias.[3] These limitations do not preclude evaluation. They simply mean that, to maintain due process, evaluation procedures must consider the weaknesses of any evidence submitted. In faculty evaluation, this requirement suggests the use of multiple techniques such as student ratings and classroom visits. The results of the multiple techniques can be compared for consistency and examined by people who are sensitive to the context of the situation and to the possible sources of bias and other errors.

Other limitations in the techniques of faculty evaluation can be dealt with by improving decision-making procedures. Many institutions have replaced vague information promotion guidelines with clearly specified decision-making procedures. To enhance due process, these procedures can be amplified to clarify institutional expectations, to apprise individuals of their strengths and weaknesses, to overcome major sources of bias in faculty evaluation, to replace bureaucratic rules with informed judgment, and to improve auditing and appeal procedures for personnel decisions.

Generalized statements about effective teaching and productive scholarship must be translated into the context of the

[1] F. Costin and others, "Student Ratings of College Teaching: Reliability, Validity, and Usefulness." *Review of Educational Research 41* (1971): 511–535.

[2] J. A. Centra, "Colleagues as Raters of Classroom Instruction," *Journal of Higher Education 46* (1975): 327–337.

[3] H. B. Sagen, "Student, Faculty, and Department Chairmen Ratings of Instructors: Who Agrees with Whom?" *Research in Higher Education 2* (1974): 265–272.

faculty member's current activities and priorities. For nontenured faculty especially, expectations must be framed in terms of time. Too often nontenured faculty are confronted with a series of short-term expectations enforced by an annual evaluation. Expectations of all faculty should be formulated in clear, reasonable, multiyear goals articulated with institutional aims and subject to revision as conditions change. Evaluation should determine the progress toward these goals and specify the steps to be taken during the next evaluation period. This procedure is now often called a "faculty growth contract," but in reality any effective faculty evaluation is a growth contract.

Faculty evaluation by its nature requires subjective judgments and can never be entirely purged of bias. But bias can be minimized. The tasks of evaluation and personnel decision making can be separated to some degree. Evaluation consists of gathering and analyzing information relative to decision making. The initial analysis of faculty personnel data can be done best by faculty peers who know the individual and the context of the activities reasonably well. Delegating functional authority for decision making to such a group, however, increases the possibility of judgments rendered on the basis of personal characteristics irrelevant to organizational goals. More effective and less biased decisions can generally be made by an individual or group somewhat removed from the immediate situation. The appropriate decision-making body, as indicated previously, should be a unit, itself accountable for decisions that contribute to organizational goals. Consideration of the immediate peer group's evaluation by a larger unit also constitutes an audit of the peer review itself.

Personnel decisions or recommendations by a department or other unit should, of course, ultimately be reviewed and ratified at the institutional level. This review establishes the framework of accountability within which evaluation of individuals is conducted and constitutes a performance audit of each unit's contribution to the institution. Establishment of a reasonable appeal and grievance procedure will further reduce charges of bias and initiates an additional review of unit-level procedures.

Although objectivity is highly desired, faculty evaluation must resist what appears to be a trend toward quantified decisions.[4] Expressing evaluative criteria and results in extremely precise form cannot improve the basic data. In fact, doing so often creates an aura of objectivity that is not justified. Objective checklists and quantified data can provide useful information to decision-makers. But data are only a basis for informed judgment; they cannot be substituted for the judgment itself. Nor can reliance on quantification absolve decision makers of the responsibility for their decisions, however well documented. Individual justice resists quantification and on occasion must overcome the rules of logic itself.

Although the relationship of individual evaluation to institutional accountability is a major issue in faculty evaluation, the most critical concern in faculty personnel matters at present is distributive justice, the policies by which the benefits and the burdens of the organization are allocated among its members. Three major inequalities prevail in current personnel policies. The first reveals not only that evaluation is more thorough for nontenured faculty, but also that the expected levels of performance are often higher. Indeed, systematic evaluation of tenured faculty may be virtually nonexistent. The second inequality is that faculty on nontenure status frequently bear a disproportionate share of the risks of falling enrollment and changing economic conditions. Third, higher expectations for faculty performance and increased demands for accountability are seldom matched by improved economic benefits. For the past several years, faculty and staff have subsidized the cost of inflation at most institutions.

Because of the long-range consequences of granting tenure and promotions, faculty evaluation has correctly emphasized a thorough and systematic assessment of nontenured faculty. In many institutions, however, full professors are not systematically appraised, particularly in the area of teaching effectiveness. Their salary increments, if related to merit at all, are based on anecdotal evidence. The argument is often made that senior faculty have demonstrated their teaching effectiveness and need not be evaluated further. In addition to the fundamental fallacy of this argument, changes in the aca-

[4]R. L. Miller, *Evaluating Faculty Performance* (San Francisco: Jossey-Bass, 1972).

demic labor market have meant that more recent faculty are often subjected to much higher standards of promotion than standards applied to older faculty when they reached the same point in their careers. If criteria for performance are to be raised, they should be raised for all faculty according to the stage of professional development achieved.

The single most significant improvement in faculty evaluation at many institutions would be to subject all faculty and, indeed, all staff to systematic evaluation of each phase of professional service. This change would not only meet the demand for accountability and improved institutional effectiveness, but it would also remove the source of inappropriate influence that tenured faculty now exert over their nontenured colleagues—influence that extends to virtually all issues within an institution. All faculty should be evaluated according to their unique contribution. Analysis of the stages of professional development among faculty[5] suggests that expectations should not be the same for the twenty-five-year-old assistant professor as for the sixty-year-old full professor. More experienced faculty often assume that expectations for new faculty should be the same as their own.

Neither the concept of tenure, which originated primarily to protect academic freedom, nor the present state of the art in faculty evaluation were designed to cope with the current dilemmas of many institutions. Tenured faculty, administrators, and the institution itself should bear a greater share of the risks of falling enrollment and changing economic conditions. At too many institutions, new faculty are added with the provision that only a small fraction, often less than one third, can expect to be given tenure. Faculty are thus asked to invest five or six years of their lives with little expectation of continued employment. Nontenured faculty should be judged against reasonable standards, and if these standards are met tenure should be awarded. To ensure flexibility in adjusting to enrollment and economic shifts, a small percentage of faculty positions should be specified as outside the tenure tract. Although tenure rates must inevitably reflect a variety of institutional

[5]H. L. Hodgkinson, "Adult Development: Implications for Faculty and Administrators," *Educational Record* 55 (1974): 263–274.

conditions, most institutions appear capable of increasing to perhaps 70 percent tenured faculty in contrast to the current national figure of 55 percent. If significant reductions in personnel become necessary, adequate staffing of basic programs will require that some tenured as well as nontenured faculty must be released. Unreasonably low tenure rates cannot be justified by the argument for institutional flexibility.

Justice for faculty further requires that faculty evaluation be linked firmly with faculty development. Many of the criticisms of faculty performance reflect changing demands for new courses and instructional methods, and for services to nontraditional students. These expectations affect some faculty more than others and those who bear the burden of new demands should be given assistance in the form of released time and other resources to develop effective instruction. Likewise, where all faculty face increased expectations, the resources necessary for improvement must be provided if equity is to be maintained.

Finally, justice in faculty evaluation will not be achieved unless economic and other rewards can be raised to levels that recognize and encourage improved performance. One of the reasons so little evaluation has been made of tenured faculty is that salary increases have not been available to keep up with inflation, let alone to be allocated on the basis of merit. Until institutions can allocate greater economic and other rewards, faculty evaluations will have little positive impact for most staff.

Systematic evaluation is the major technique by which educational institutions may be accountable to students and society. Evaluation is also an inexact and subjective art practiced by fallible human beings using techniques of limited value. The decisions rendered have an enormous impact on fellow human beings who have invested much of their lives preparing for educational service. Recognition of these conditions will not make evaluation any easier, but it should make personnel practices more humane and more effective.

Disciplinary Associations and Faculty Development

Myron A. Marty

Ironies and contradictions spring to the foreground when one considers the role of disciplinary associations in faculty development. Faculty development is intended to improve the *teaching* of *individuals* in *institutional* settings. Disciplinary organizations are *research* oriented, are largely concerned with *group* interests, and are *professional* and *suprainstitutional* in character. To a certain extent, disciplinary associations are characterized by the very practices faculty development programs attempt to change.

Consider, for example, a disciplinary association's annual meeting. By its isolation from other disciplines, it separates its members, if only momentarily, from the real world of higher education. Lectures, called "papers," are read, usually too fast and often in a monotone. Rarely are they enlivened, enriched, or reinforced by the use of electronic media. Listeners sit in straight and often crowded rows. The responses to these lectures are also read, and it is not surprising when they fail to deal with the substance of the lectures. After all, having the floor in one of these sessions seems to carry the prerogative of presenting the findings of one's latest research regardless of its relevance to the theme of the session. Discussion follows the formal responses. Again, those who speak up are as likely to unload what is on their minds as they are to confront the thesis and the evidence of the presenter. The lectures themselves are often noteworthy for their narrowness or for their esoteric quality. Because they are designed by specialists for specialists, there is a high premium on protecting intellectual flanks—a maneuver often performed by shrouding arguments in studied opacity. The narrowness of the topics reduces the likelihood that the research that went into preparing the papers had much impact on the presenter's teaching. Perhaps the time spent in preparation was time that might better have been devoted to getting ready for classroom duties. This is not to say, of course, that all of the papers on specialized topics are useless, or even that most of them are, or that preparing and presenting them does not contribute to the professional growth of the presenter. For some presenters and some hearers, this mode of advancing and disseminating knowledge may serve good purposes. It seems useful, though, to ask whether the dividends of such papers are commensurate with the investment of time and energy they require.

Although the program emphasis is on the evidence and fruits of scholarly research, various associations have in recent years included a few sessions on teaching. In liveliness and utility, the presentations in these sessions bear a strong resemblance to those with a research theme. Sometimes they are little more than jeremiads, bemoaning the condition of the discipline in the classroom without offering constructive suggestions for improving it. The appearance in these sessions of big names in the discipline is rare. If demonstrations or workshops on teaching are offered, as they seem to be with increasing frequency, they are likely to be at inconvenient times and in remote places.

The journals of disciplinary organizations appear to be even less concerned with teaching. The overwhelming majority of the members who receive these journals have teaching as their principal responsibility. Yet, penetrating the pages of the journals with an article dealing with teaching is practically unheard of. Scholarly purity is maintained, even if the articles are widely unread.

This description of disciplinary associations is not offered as disparaging criticism. As they have defined their purposes, they are doing a good job. But if they are going to contribute to faculty development as that term is now understood, they will have to change directions, adopt new purposes, and cultivate new emphases. As I shall show later, this can be done. In fact, in a number of organizations changes have already begun to occur.

Faculty development, broadly defined, is not a new invention. It was once called *professional growth,* and it referred to self-initiated efforts by faculty members to increase their general competence, to improve their effectiveness as teachers, to extend themselves into new areas, to contribute to humankind's knowledge and understanding of the world in which it lives, and to produce published evidence of scholarly craftsmanship. In some cases, probably many of them, institutional incentives stimulated the last of these through sanctions and rewards. If faculty development is understood as professional growth, Richard Kirkendall, executive secretary of the Organization of American Historians, is correct when he says, "Everything we do is aimed at faculty development. All of the activities and committees and publications of the organization are designed to aid professional growth."[1] Bennett Wall of the Southern Historical Association indicates a similar understanding when he says that although that organization has, in a formal sense, no agency or committee actively engaged in fostering or promoting faculty development, "the secretary-treasurers and the program chairmen of this association would support my statement that we have constantly sought to upgrade the historical profession."[2]

[1] Personal conversation with R. Kirkendall at the University of Chicago on January 17, 1976.
[2] Letter from B. Wall to author, January 28, 1976.

But faculty development, narrowly defined, must be described with precision: it embraces organized, systematic, comprehensive efforts to improve the performance of faculty members *as teachers*. Based on the assumption that a faculty member's principal task is to teach, it stresses the need to perceive and cultivate relationships between personal career needs, instructional obligations, and institutional demands. Faculty development compels teachers—professors included—to come to new understandings of themselves and their institutions.

Faculty self-satisfaction and complacency, even complacency abetted by weariness, are likely to be challenged only when the circumstances that have fostered them have changed. The realization of changed circumstances, although it has been slow in coming, is beginning to sink in. Declining enrollments, competition for students, the end of money to support research projects, the end of faculty mobility, calls for accountability by parents and legislators, pressure for reform by alumni and discontented students—all of these changes are part of higher education's new environment. Some teachers can remain happily or unhappily oblivious to the current plight of higher education and to the potentially dismal prospects for their role in it. Others experience what William Bergquist and Steven Phillips call an "unfreezing." Flushed by feelings of discrepancy, dissonance, pain, or stress, they open themselves to the new ideas faculty development seemingly holds for them. Without the unfreezing experience, they would either resist faculty development or take part in it so listlessly that they would not be affected by it.[3]

How do disciplinary organizations fit into this picture of faculty development? First, they can sensitize their members to the problems of higher education in general and of their disciplines in particular, and thus can contribute to the unfreezing process that makes faculty members receptive to faculty development. Second, by conferring an enlarged sense of legitimacy on teaching as distinct from research, they can make it respectable for their members to participate in programs aimed at increasing effectiveness in the classroom. Third, they can

[3]W. H. Bergquist and S. R. Phillips, "Components of an Effective Faculty Development Program," *Journal of Higher Education 46* (March–April 1975): p. 185.

offer positive assistance to faculty development programs, in
some cases providing the initiative, support, and direction that
make the difference between success and failure.

But any assessment of the prospects for notable contributions by disciplinary associations to faculty development must
be made with several limitations in mind. Their members are a
diverse lot: interests and responsibilities vary according to professional situations; different reasons for membership prompt
differing expectations of benefits to be gained from it; enthusiasm for the association's purposes and pride of membership
ranges from intense to indifferent. The American Historical
Association (AHA) numbers about 15,000; the Organization of
American Historians (OAH), 8,500; the American Sociological
Association (ASA), about 15,000. How does one mobilize organizations of such size? Furthermore, even with such numbers,
their financial resources are limited. Their members are scat-
tered around the country and immersed in their own work;
it is hard for them to maintain a close relationship with a national organization. Quarterly meetings cannot accomplish
much, and more frequent meetings are out of the question for
most members.

Despite these limitations, disciplinary associations can
make a valuable contribution to faculty development. The employment crisis that has hit some disciplines particularly hard
has raised consciousness and increased sensitivity among faculty
members as nothing else could have. But it did not provide understanding. That comes, if it comes at all, through such thoughtful analyses as Richard Kirkendall's report, "The Status of
History in the Schools." Published by OAH, this report has had
considerable impact on both the profession and the general
public.[4] Stephen Graubard's essay in the November 1975 *AHA
Newsletter* is another example of an attempt to help historians
understand their own illnesses in the light of the general malaise
of higher education. That essay is a commentary from the historian's perspective on the two *Daedalus* issues that Graubard
edited, *American Higher Education: Toward an Uncertain Future*
(Fall 1974, Winter 1975). No doubt other disciplinary associations have followed similar sensitization measures.

[4] *Journal of American History LXII* (September 1975): 557–570.

Conferring legitimacy on teaching requires a greater commitment on the part of the association than does sensitizing people to problems. That it is being tried structurally is shown by the existence within the American Sociological Association of the Council on Undergraduate Teaching, and by the recent establishment within the American Historical Association of a teaching division headed by one of the three AHA vice presidents. This division, which is in effect a consolidation of some long-standing interests, aims "to collect and disseminate information about the training of teachers and about instructional techniques and materials and to encourage excellence in the teaching of history in the schools, colleges, and universities."[5] Perhaps the most visible creation of this division has been the column on teaching, now in its second year, in the monthly *AHA Newsletter*.

Conference sessions on teaching also help confer legitimacy. The extent to which they do so, however, may be limited because those who attend these sessions are likely to be the people who have no problem with the legitimacy of teaching. This clustering effect—with those who support faculty development in one camp and those who resist it in another—presents a real problem. The members of each group are not only reinforced in their views by their fellows, they are inclined to be scornful of those in the other camp. To the extent to which this is happening, teaching and research, which theoretically are mutually supportive, have become polarized.

To deal with this problem the disciplinary associations have an obligation, in my judgment, to study the relationship between teaching and research and to show that neither should be ignored at the expense of the other. There is a difference between a history teacher and a historian and between a sociology teacher and a sociologist. Research pursuits may not make one a better teacher, but they do make one a different kind of teacher. How both teachers and scholars can learn to understand their limitations and make better use of their resources is a matter the associations would do well to explore.[6]

[5]American Historical Association Constitution, Article 6, Section 3.
[6]I have looked into these questions in "Historical Research and the Community College Teacher: Refreshment on the Side Roads," *The History Teacher* (February 1975): 217–228.

The increased attention given to the teaching of history is in part a consequence of the formation of an independent society devoted to promoting history education and of the appearance of a "teaching lobby" within the AHA. Whether the Society for History Education (SHE), publisher since 1972 of an excellent journal called *The History Teacher,* should come into some sort of alliance with the OAH and the AHA has been under discussion for some time. The Committee on History in the Classroom (CHC), organized as a rump group several years ago, was recently granted AHA-affiliate status. To my knowledge, neither the SHE nor the CHC has undertaken anything that might be considered faculty development, but they are both favorably disposed toward anything the major associations might undertake to promote improved teaching.

Legitimacy is also conferred by commitment, and commitment shows itself in specific efforts to bring about improved teaching. One such effort is a pilot project in faculty development in which the American Historical Association has been involved since 1973. This project, the Long Island Faculty Development Program, involves history teachers and historians from State University of New York (SUNY) at Stony Brook, SUNY Agricultural and Technical College at Farmingdale, Nassau Community College, and the two campuses of Suffolk Community College. According to Mack Thompson, executive director of the AHA, two main lessons have been learned from the project. First, an extraordinary amount of time, effort, and commitment on the part of project directors and participants is necessary to begin a process of change and improvement of teaching. A national organization can assist in developing guidelines, identifying and recruiting personnel, securing outside funding, administering grants, and disseminating information about the project to a national audience, but the success or failure of the project is in the hands of the participants. Second, interinstitutional cooperation, which is especially valuable among different types of institutions, is greatly enhanced by the channels of communication opened by faculty development efforts.

Working with persons from the Long Island Program and the American Association of Community and Junior Colleges, Thompson has drafted an impressive proposal for increased AHA involvement in faculty development. The proposal states flatly that the AHA "now seeks to redefine its priorities and to reassert the leadership of history in the process of educational reform."[7] The proposal emphasizes many of the features of the Long Island Program. Among the more significant ones are these: that faculty development programs should be planned *by* the participants *for* the participants; that programs should have a clear focus and participants should have clearly stated sets of objectives; that the programs should be operated cooperatively by institutions with some clearly identified common bond; that they should be designed to become eventually part of the regular institutional operating budgets; that they should be organized around a "community-of-peers" principle; and that they should include varieties of activities that focus on concrete issues such as grading, evaluation, and the production of teaching materials.

The proposal gives this description of goals: "This five-year program of faculty development will create permanent mechanisms for educational reform in colleges and universities across the country. It will improve the performance and effectiveness of individual faculty members in a variety of institutions and teaching situations. It will provide teachers with a disciplinary-based vehicle for change and a structured way of interacting with students and administrators who also seek reform. It directly attacks the lack of articulation between two- and four-year institutions. And finally, it provides ways in which the AHA and other disciplinary organizations can readjust their functions to serve their constituencies more effectively." These are praiseworthy goals. If the American Historical Association can generate support for them among its members and if it can muster the financial support for their achievement, a major milestone in American education will have been reached.

A major milestone has already been reached by the American Sociological Association. In 1974 the ASA undertook the

[7]Materials used in this section were kindly provided by AHA Executive Secretary Mack Thompson. They included: "The AHA and Faculty Development," Thompson's presentation at the AHA meeting on December 28, 1975, in Atlanta, Georgia; "American Historical Association Proposal for a National Program of Faculty Development," unpublished and undated staff working paper, Washington, D.C.; and "The American Historical Association Proposal to the Lilly Endowment: For Renewal of Faculty Development Program," May 23, 1975, Washington, D.C. It should be understood that the role of the AHA in faculty development is an evolving one. Future documents will reflect what has been learned by experience at each stage.

sponsorship of a massive project titled, "A Program of Assessment, Articulation, and Experimentation in Undergraduate Teaching of Sociology in the United States." Supported by a grant from the Fund for the Improvement of Post-Secondary Education, this project is working through three task groups— one to explore the content, organization, and objectives of the sociology curriculum; another to consider the skills and the development and maintenance of competence of teachers; and a third to examine the institutional conditions under which sociology is taught. The project has sought to improve ties between sociology teachers in community colleges and their counterparts in four-year institutions. One result of this effort is the establishment of a national network of persons dedicated to more effective sociology teaching.

The project is attempting to link the activities of its three task groups to a broad program of experimentation, evaluation, and dissemination. The long-range goals of the project are: to develop criteria for judging the quality, sophistication, and disciplinary rigor of undergraduate programs in sociology; to develop an information program that will allow faculty to locate resources and exchange ideas on undergraduate teaching; to stimulate the interest and involvement of sociology teachers in professional growth, particularly in those institutions that are not in the mainstream of sociological scholarship and research; to establish a pattern of experimentation and evaluation in the teaching process; to encourage the use of the most advanced capabilities of the discipline in the undergraduate curriculum; and to institutionalize, through these efforts, the commitment of the profession to undergraduate education and to those institutions whose primary activity is the teaching of undergraduates.

Although this is a three-year project, its aim is to keep its impact going through the ASA in subsequent years. This challenge will test the resources and the commitment of the association. If the challenge is met, it will significantly alter the ASA.

If nothing else, these emerging efforts demonstrate an earnest desire on the part of *some* disciplinary associations to play an active role in faculty development. Whether the associations increase their commitment will depend not only on their leadership but also on their membership. People can be helped in their teaching only to the extent that they are willing to learn.

9

Professional Development for Women

Janet Welsh Brown

Any discussion of women in higher education must consider several different groups of women. In the field of professional development, discussions usually center on faculty women and, to a lesser extent, on lower- and middle-level administrators. An even larger group, which includes women teachers, researchers, and administrative assistants, has received little attention. These women are least likely to be found at professional meetings, are least likely to be organized, and are often exploited and forgotten. Women students are another neglected group that deserves consideration. Their campus experiences are often a bellwether of the status of all women on the campus.

There are two ways of looking at the current status of women in higher education or anywhere else: the male point of view and the female point of view. This is clearly an over-simplification, for there are some women who share the male point of view and, fortunately, some men who share the women's point of view. Nevertheless, most men perceive that progress for women is taking place rapidly. Some are proud of that progress and some are troubled by the continued demands of women. The women, on the other hand, perceive endless talk, a semblance of activity, and precious little progress. They are increasingly impatient and dissatisfied.

One can find illustrations of these points of view in practically any field. At a recent joint meeting of women in the labor movement and women in professional organizations,[1] a representative of the American Federation of Television and Radio Artists noted the increased share of "voice-overs" (the voice of "authority" in a television commercial) going to women. In just a few years the women's share of these assignments had increased from 3 percent to 6 percent The men in the profession consider this a 100 percent increase. What is significant to women is that men still get 94 percent of the jobs.

In higher education, the difference in these points of view is also easily illustrated. At the National Conference on Higher Education, National Institute of Education Director Harold Hodgkinson referred to the women's share in graduate and professional enrollments over the decades.[2] He drew attention to the fact that women's share of those enrollments increased sharply, and briefly, during World War II, reflecting a national commitment during those years to women's education. That is the man's point of view. (Dr. Hodgkinson made light of the implications: if you want to increase women's participation, send the men off to war.) I interpreted the data he presented quite differently—noting that the percentage of women enrolled in graduate schools in the mid-seventies is

[1]Women's Conference, sponsored by the Federation of Organizations for Professional Women and the Committee on Salaried and Professional Women/AFL-CIO, AFL-CIO Labor Studies Center, Silver Spring, Maryland, February 2–3, 1976.

[2]H. L. Hodgkinson, "The Legislative Process as Seen by the New Director of the National Institute of Education," 31st National Conference on Higher Education, Chicago, March 9, 1976.

the same as it was in 1910. That is the women's point of view.

Ladd and Lipset, in the first paragraphs of a recent article on faculty women, illustrate clearly the male-female points of view.[3] They point out that since 1969 the percentage of women on faculties in the United States has increased from 19 percent to 21 percent. They first refer to this as "striking gains." Apparently, one third of one percent per year is a lot of progress in a tight market. That is the male point of view. Then they go on to say that women occupy very much the same status as before—which I would label the women's point of view. Their summary points out that women spend more time teaching than men, earn less, are less involved in publishing, and are segregated by rank, discipline, and type of institution where they teach.

The same Ladd-Lipset survey tells us that a record one third of faculty members under thirty years of age are women. These women may be the most vulnerable group of employees in higher education today. What will happen to them if the current patterns and trends persist? There will be only delicate shifts in most institutions, with a few more women receiving promotions than in the past, but in general the current patterns will persist: fewer women than men will be promoted, fewer will be found in the prestigious institutions, fewer will have research opportunities, and more will be unemployed.[4]

This dismal picture will change only when universities and colleges recognize how far we have to go to reach equality, not how far we have come. When most of the men who control most of the institutions of higher education can admit that the educational system has favored and still favors men over women, the rate of improvement will quicken. The tensions between the

[3]E. C. Ladd and S. M. Lipset, "Faculty Women: Little Gains in Status," *Chronicle of Higher Education*, September 29, 1975: 2.

[4]There are myths abroad in the land that women and minority Ph.D.s have it made these days, that they get hired first and paid more than white male colleagues. That simply is not so except in a handful of cases. The National Academy of Science's *Summary Report on 1974 Doctorate Recipients* (Washington, D.C.: National Academy of Science, June 1975) shows that in *every* field women Ph.D.s (and black, Indian, and Asian Ph.D.s of both sexes) were still unemployed and seeking positions in higher proportions than white males. The same was true for women seeking postdoctoral appointments, except in engineering, pp. 7,9.

two points of view will become creative tensions only when the women's point of view is recognized as valid.

It is becoming increasingly popular these days to believe that federal interference is diminishing the quality of higher education in the United States.[5] Many of the complaints of universities concern federally required procedures and reports relating to affirmative action. These complaints have been articulated by Kingman Brewster of Yale,[6] Philip Abelson of *Science* magazine,[7] and Thomas Sowell of the University of California at Los Angeles.[8] Sowell delivers the coup de grace with his suggestion that affirmative action may have done more harm than good. This is surely the man's point of view. This implied opposition between quality and equality is nonsense. There cannot be quality without equality. Academic excellence requires diversity to assure that ideas, values, and assumptions are constantly challenged. A monolithic community runs the risk of complacency, smugness, and actual error.

There is great resistance among academics to the idea that personal values, the values instilled by class and education, shape one's scholarship, teaching, and administration. Most social scientists do not like to admit the extent to which their value systems affect their professional life, and some natural scientists are actually offended by the suggestion that their science is value shaded. This is still the case in spite of the efforts of some scholars, notably Margaret Mead, who recognize cultural bias in all science.[9]

The exclusion of women from the powerful research and decision-making circles of intellectual life has seriously impaired the quality of our science. One way in which quality has been affected is in the selection of research areas and pri-

[5]See also N. Epstein, "Academic Hypocrisy: A Media View," elsewhere in this volume.

[6]K. Brewster, speech given before the Fellows of the American Bar Foundation, 22 February 1975, and excerpted for an editorial, "Coercive Power of the Federal Purse," *Science 188*, April 11, 1975, p. 105.

[7]P. H. Abelson, "Federal Intervention in the Universities," *Science 190* October 17, 1975, p. 221.

[8]T. Sowell, *Affirmative Action Reconsidered: Was it Necessary in Academia?* (Washington, D.C.: American Enterprise Institute for Public Policy Research, 1975).

[9]M. Mead, "Anthropologists, Scientists and Laity," *The Sciences,* Nov.–Dec. 1967, 7 (Nos. 6 and 7), 10–13.

orities. A recent example was relayed to me by a biologist who attended a meeting of developmental biologists and heard a report on the genetic manipulation involved in the formation of a single mouse with four parents.[10] The researchers reported that they had genetically identified a kind of sterility in mice caused by the absence of a receptor for testosterone. Thus, even if the testosterone is supplied from the normal set of parents, the mutant parent cannot make sperm. A member of the audience noted the potential importance of this finding for the development of male contraceptives and inquired whether that possibility was being investigated. The answer came without hesitation: "Oh no, none of my male research assistants would be interested in working on that!"

The point to be drawn from this anecdote is that without a healthy mix of women and minorities in the academic world, many values and assumptions will remain unchallenged. Seen in this light, affirmative action is not only a moral and legal responsibility; it is also an intellectual responsibility affecting the quality of education and research in our universities.

People in higher education, like any other endeavor, tend to follow the paths that are most familiar to them. We continue to assign term papers because we know the value of doing one. We stick to the tried and true lecture method even though we suspect that other teaching methods might engage our students' interests more successfully. We appoint people we know and can work with to committees. We go to lunch with colleagues we enjoy rather than with those who might question our assumptions. But if universities are to fulfill their function of preserving and advancing knowledge, if they are to become places of quality, we have to step off these paths of least resistance and experience a little discomfort, intellectually and emotionally. We have to be willing to encounter a constant questioning of our assumptions. This is the very basis of the scientific, intellectual life of the university, and it can be assured only with diversity. This dependency of quality on diversity is perhaps the compelling intellectual argument for equality—for the inclusion, promotion, and advancement of people who are different.

[10]C. L. Markert, "Biological Nature of Communication: Finding a Mate," paper presented at the New England Regional Developmental Biology Conference, Boston, Massachusetts, Feb. 20, 1976.

But no matter how compelling the case for increasing the participation of women in higher education, few gains will be made without work at the practical level. This means not only efforts to recruit and promote more women but, less obviously, a variety of changes to assure better professional development for women. A logical place to begin making such changes is in the education college women receive.

To make education work for women as well as it does for men, institutions need to give attention to three problems: sex segregation by discipline, the serious difference in dropout rates between men and women graduate students, and sexually stereotyped placement assistance for graduates. Only in a few institutions are these problems being addressed seriously. We know from the experience of institutions as different as the Massachusetts Institute of Technology and Spelman that women can be attracted into fields traditionally dominated by men. We know that a different kind of encouragement from faculty could increase the proportion of women science majors going on to graduate school. We know from the experience of a number of institutions that the supportive services of a well-staffed women's center can lower the dropout rate of women in graduate schools. We know that adequate, de-sexed counseling and placement services can make a difference in the positions women get and that corporations will hire women in the same positions as men.

To put this knowledge into practice on a large scale will require changing behaviors and attitudes, and that is not easy to do. The university administration must take the responsibility for developing systems, checks, and assessments that everyone will have to follow. This means, first of all, that the institution must study and monitor its own progress. A commission on the status of women in the institution should be formed to do so. The commission should be adequately supported and should include students, faculty, staff, and administrators. Its responsibilities should be to evaluate and then to monitor efforts to achieve equal opportunity. It must have status, clout, direct access to the president, and the cooperation of all departments. Its recommendations must be followed and the results assessed annually. There are some fine models of commissions on the status of women,[11] but most institutions have ignored them, relying instead on an affirmative action officer. One person is not enough. Although affirmative action officers know how many women have been admitted or how many are on the faculty, they cannot keep track of what is happening to the women in the institution.

Women's centers and women's studies programs are two additional mechanisms for achieving equal opportunity. The centers provide needed psychological and intellectual support, and the women's studies programs stimulate interest in women's problems, increase knowledge about those problems, and lead to research in areas affecting women. There is a good bit of skepticism about the necessity for women's studies. They are often compared with black studies, which have come under heavy criticism. But black studies did not fail. Some programs are thriving as centers of scholarship. Others, often more political and sometimes less scholarly, have disappeared, but not without accomplishing such valuable goals as raising levels of awareness, getting black Americans back into history, and getting black authors onto required reading lists. Black studies have provided psychological and intellectual support for black students. Women's studies are needed to do the same for women students. Along with the centers, they can be powerful agents for creating change.

The foregoing suggestions are concerned with the education of women. The prime, but not sole, beneficiaries of such measures would be women students. A second area where work is needed is in providing opportunities and experiences that can enrich the professional life of women. Here the immediate beneficiaries would be women faculty, staff, and administrators.

Young faculty are in a tight bind these days. Universities are top-heavy with tenured faculty and expansion is not a feasible way of providing mobility for the untenured. Consequently,

[11]See, for instance, *Today and Tomorrow: Annual Report of The Commission on the Status of Women* (Detroit: Wayne State University, 1972) or *The Status of Women Graduate and Professional Students at the University of Washington over the Past Decade,* a report by the Committee for the Recruitment and Counselling of Women Graduate and Professional Students, University of Washington, March 1, 1974.

most of these young people, male and female, are going to be
released before they achieve tenure. Many will leave the academic world. What the university does to train them will in great
measure decide whether they reach the nonacademic world
with marketable skills. Teaching skills—the ones most likely
to be acquired—will not help them much. Research experience
may, but most likely it is the administrative skills that will be
most transferable. To help women develop such skills, universities should expand opportunities for them to attend professional meetings, serve on committees, work on budgets, learn
computer programing, write books, or take part in bargaining
sessions. Through such experiences, women can gain not only
skills and knowledge but the exposure, contacts, and references
necessary for mobility and survival. Institutions could increase
the participation of women in these activities in a number of
ways: by rewarding such participation, by providing release
time to take part in them, by arranging part-time or temporary
job assignments, and by encouraging senior faculty and administrators to serve as mentors to those who are less experienced.
All too often the people who most need experience are the least
likely to get it. Firm policies and determined leadership can
change that.

Another form of experience needed to improve the status of academic women is training. This includes university
and government internships, leaves of absence to work on task
forces, in professional societies, and in exchanges with industry,
and participation in summer programs in educational administration such as those run by the Harvard Business School and
the American Council on Education. Women and minorities
have much to learn from these training opportunities. They
also can benefit from less expensive and increasingly common
programs designed specifically for women—programs that
teach them the skills and confidence they lack. Universities
should sponsor promising women leaders for such opportunities as they have done for men.

These special opportunities for women and minorities
will not only help make up for past discrimination; they will
help eliminate discriminatory practices and attitudes that continue to pervade institutional behavior. Self-examination at

most institutions will reveal at least three respects in which women regularly get treated differently from men on the job.

First, women often fill responsible positions without being given appropriate titles and authority, so their resumes and job descriptions are not accurate reflections of job experience. In universities women are often secretaries of committees rather than chairpersons, though they might be the real leaders. Similarly, women research assistants sometimes actually run research projects for the primary investigators. Though they may be conditioned to accept their status unquestioningly, they more often do so through lack of alternatives.

Second, when women do get promoted, they are treated differently from men entering similar positions. They are seldom protected by patrons and usually have to sink or swim on their own. Their promotion to a new position does not mean automatic access to new networks. Instead, lacking the support of male colleagues, women have to develop their own networks of support.

Third, women and minorities are assessed differently on the job. Strong leadership is quickly criticized as being too aggressive. On the other hand, if a woman's administrative style is informal or relaxed, she may be characterized as "soft," and regarded as a poor manager.

One additional problem shared by women and minorities deserves mention. Because they are a relatively scarce commodity, academic women and minorities often receive token appointments to committees (in which they may or may not have an interest) and are required to advise colleagues on women and minority problems (in which they are always assumed to have an interest). Minority women find these obligations doubly burdensome.[12] Most women and minority faculty bear the extra burden of advising women and minority students and faculty who come to them. They seldom receive recognition or compensation for the extra hours and the additional psychological burdens. Institutions badly need this kind of help for their

[12]S. S. Malcolm, P. Q. Hall, and J. W. Brown, *The Double Bind: The Price of Being a Minority Woman in Science* (Washington, D.C.: American Association for the Advancement of Science, 1976).

women and minority students, but it should be reasonably sched-
uled and properly rewarded.

   The complaints of women in higher education are real
and numerous. Universities are not the only, and probably not
the worst, offenders, but to find that such practices abound in
the academic world is especially discouraging. Perhaps what is
needed is an additional kind of affirmative action in higher
education, one that has no numerical goals and is not enforce-
able by any federal agency but only by the institutions themselves. If the lingering sexism that impedes the professional
development of women is cleared away, if the same kind of effort is made for women that has been made for majority males
in the past, the need for federal enforcement will gradually
disappear.

10

A Case Study in Faculty Development

J. Herman Blake
Ronald W. Saufley

Oakes College is one of eight liberal arts colleges on the campus of the University of California, Santa Cruz. Like other colleges on campus, Oakes has its own unique interests with corresponding curricular and extracurricular programs, but its students also take courses throughout the university and can major in any of twenty-two campuswide disciplines. The result is a coupling of the best of two worlds—the intimate relationships of a small residential college with its own intellectual and moral environment directly reflecting the interests of its members, and the immediate availability of the resources of a great university.

Among the specific goals of Oakes College are the provision of equal educational opportunity within the framework of a culturally unbiased academic atmosphere and the develop-

97

ment of a community morality based on universal human concerns. The college is in the process of developing a diverse, multiethnic collegiate community founded on the development of intercultural perspectives that include recognition and acceptance of the *validity* of human diversity, and the realization that a human community with unifying human values gains exceptional strength from the variety of cultural and biological variations implicit in the human experience.

From its inception, Oakes College has been committed to equal educational opportunity in practice as well as in theory. The student body is currently comprised of over 30 percent minority students, with the number rising each year. (We currently have approximately 525 students, with an ultimate projection of 700 students at full growth.) We also have a significant number of white students from backgrounds of extreme poverty.

Among the various groups of "nontraditional" students, some, of course, are totally qualified for university work; a good many others bring academic problems that require considerable extra effort. Regardless of preparation, however, there is one significant common denominator among nearly all of the "nontraditional" students: when they enter the university they have considerable concern as to whether they belong—as a result of guilt feelings about leaving the home community and using valuable family resources for their educations, or a sense of alienation and isolation, or simply not understanding how they relate to the university experience.

Oakes recognizes that programs alone—no matter how effectively developed—are incapable of dealing with certain psychological or preparation problems of various students. Students often need faculty members with whom they can not only relate, but identify. Such faculty members serve not only as role models or as symbolic statements of the possible, but their immediate concern and support of troubled students is often the deciding factor in a student's finally making an effective bridge between his or her background and the college experience.

As a direct consequence of its philosophies, the college from the beginning assiduously recruited highly qualified ethnic faculty, women, white faculty from poverty backgrounds, as

well as more traditional faculty members. Our current regular
faculty of twenty-eight is comprised of 50 percent minority
members—Chicano, black, Asian, and Puerto Rican—and includes eight women. These faculty were not recruited merely to
provide a temporary presence or to teach in special programs,
they are "on-ladder" faculty members on the normal tenure
track in the university. They are all eminently qualified teachers
and scholars who meet the rigorous standards of the University
of California, and they are faculty extremely sensitive and responsive to the new student constituency that has such diverse
backgrounds.

Since the college opened in 1972, Oakes has been extremely fortunate in securing a dedicated faculty willing to work
closely together to develop coherent college programs from
scratch and to develop new teaching approaches geared to the
diverse student body we are serving. Yet from the beginning,
we have recognized that the faculty's very commitment to the
college and to students could result in their own—and ultimately the college's—destruction.

The University of California is still primarily a publish-
or-perish institution, and as a new college, Oaks has a predominantly young and untenured faculty. The exceptional amount
of time involved in mounting college efforts—planning and
teaching in new programs and real interdisciplinary courses,
trying to know *each* student in a class in order to build on individual strengths and overcome individual weaknesses, and
the willingness to pursue research in areas related to pedagogy
as well as to pursue traditional research—has been and could
continue to be detrimental in terms of the faculty members'
own scholarly development.

In addition to the time demands faced by all our faculty,
ethnic faculty face additional pressures that are far too often
overlooked in most institutions of higher education. So much
of their time is consumed by ethnic students in search of role
models, identity, validation, counseling, or just the need to
talk to a "brother" or "sister" about academic or personal problems. (Sometimes the students cannot articulate exactly why
they need to rap—they just do.) A related but seldom mentioned problem is the need of so many liberal white students

for catharsis that they feel can be reached by rapping with ethnic faculty. Also, on a campuswide basis, ethnic faculty members are "committeed" to death for obvious reasons.

A careful review of our initial complement of faculty compounded our concerns. At a time when we needed to develop programs and pursue pedagogical issues, our faculty was overwhelmingly junior (there were only two tenured faculty in our initial contingent—still, only seven of our faculty are now tenured), a large proportion of our faculty were still writing dissertations (to date, eleven of twenty-eight faculty have joined Oakes without the Ph.D. completed—nine have since finished), and a large percentage were women and minority group members who would face extra pressures within the system. From these characteristics we discerned several needs that became initial goals of our faculty development program.

The first goal was to ensure that those faculty who were writing dissertations had the encouragement and *opportunity* to finish. Secondly, faculty had to be protected from so many of the extraneous pressures that are found at Santa Cruz: excessive committee work and administrative responsibilities generated by the dual structures of colleges and boards of studies, extraordinary tutorial responsibilities, and counseling (as opposed to academic advising) of students with problems or identification needs. Thirdly, faculty would have to get the support and encouragement that would lead them to pursue research and publication so they could establish their professional careers. Fourthly, there had to be a continuing discussion and review of pedagogical issues and curriculum development so that the scholarly work of faculty could be more effectively transmitted to students and meet student needs.

If we were to succeed, it seemed imperative to reach *all* these goals or we would be caught in a familiar trap: seeking basic institutional change, we needed extraordinary faculty commitment; yet such commitment could lead to insufficient academic research or failure to complete dissertations, both of which were imperative if we were to retain faculty dedicated to an institutional reordering of priorities. In building programs and seeking new ways to approach a new student clientele, we were running the risk of destroying the involved faculty members, ultimately committing collegiate suicide in the process.

Thus, although our goals did not constitute a complete faculty development program, they came to form the general outline through which we developed our strategies for faculty development and survival.

The first procedure developed was to give individual faculty release-time from teaching in the college. This was done with the recognition that Oakes would be able to call on them more fully in the future. Faculty remained on campus during the release quarter(s) and performed certain necessary college functions (for example, academic advising, faculty meetings) but were relieved of all college teaching and administrative and committee assignments. The freed time was spent attending to the particular matter most affecting that faculty member: dissertation completion, necessary disciplinary research, or the planning of specific courses and programs requested by the college.

Admittedly, the unique nature of the Santa Cruz campus—with its bifurcation of colleges and boards of studies—made it less difficult to release faculty than might have been the case at other institutions. However, we would argue that the documented excessive proliferation of courses on so many campuses indicates that there is the real possibility that a release time program, requiring no additional costs, can be developed at many institutions in the United States.

The second strategy developed was a flexible teaching load—not flexibility in terms of fewer courses, but flexibility as to when courses are offered. Traditionally, faculty at the University of California are expected to teach and carry on research projects throughout the academic year. To us, however, such expectations seemed illogical if blindly followed across the board.

Although, as we have explained in detail above, we see no ultimate conflict between teaching and research, there are times when a temporary dichotomy between the two can hinder either function. At certain critical times during a research project, it is often imperative that 100 percent effort be given to the project. Conversely, there are times in teaching when one needs to devote oneself fully to that function: for example, when planning new programs, or when experimenting with new pedagogical techniques, which demand an unusually heavy course load in order to adequately conduct experimentation while maintaining sufficient control groups.

In response to this dilemma, the college periodically allowed selected faculty to rearrange their teaching schedules so that their entire course loads were taught during two of the three academic quarters, leaving the third quarter free for other activities. With the summer added to the third quarter, some faculty were able to have six consecutive months for research or dissertation completion without any loss of college programs.

Again, we would argue that many institutions could greatly enhance faculty development at no additional costs by simply building greater flexibility into the system.

The first major cost-associated strategy that the college developed was a summer salary program for all junior and some senior faculty. The college required the development of new and innovative curricular offerings and teaching strategies if we were to fulfill our missions. However, to ask faculty to develop such programs on a part-time basis, during the academic year, when they were already under considerable pressure, would greatly overload the faculty and would at the same time result in superficial offerings.

Several Oakes programs, for example, were projected to be interdisciplinary. From years of experience on the Santa Cruz campus (which prides itself on its capacity to develop such programs), we have discovered that truly successful interdisciplinary efforts require far more, rather than less, faculty time in course preparation, in communication during the course, and in necessary follow-up. We concluded, therefore, that the major portion of the planning must be done during summer, when the faculty were free of teaching and administrative responsibilities and could more easily balance program development efforts with ongoing research.

Such a conclusion, however, dictated that we secure outside resources to pay faculty for their summer efforts. With assistance from five Regent's grants, a Ford Foundation grant, and two small grants from a private individual, we were able during our first three years of operation to give every junior faculty member summer support. Occasionally, outside consultants were employed to assist in the planning effort.

In certain cases, also, faculty were given college monies for tutorial and teaching-assistant support, as well as for travel relevant both to their research and planning for Oakes courses and programs. Although the amount was very small, it was another manifestation of the commitment of the college to helping young faculty deal with the major issues facing them.

Special assistance for junior faculty in planning and writing grant proposals was provided by the college. A staff member was made available to assist faculty in any and all phases of funding their ideas. In some cases where Oakes faculty have received grants, all of the proposal writing was done by staff.

Where appropriate and possible, administrative staff have called on funding sources on behalf of particular faculty. This has been done during administrative trips to the East Coast when extra time has been taken by the provost and assistant provost to call on various agencies with faculty proposals before them, or when faculty have requested specific information regarding a funding agency's policies and programs.

In response to college and faculty concerns regarding pedagogical issues, evaluation of faculty, and the need to stimulate greater colleagueship among the faculty, Oakes College established several new intellectual forums that have been quite successful in stimulating faculty in new directions. These include a pedagogy task force; an evaluative forum for the discussion every other year of each faculty member's professional development; and divisional forums designed not to discuss "business," but to explore areas of mutual interest.

The pedagogy task force, in addition to conducting and disseminating educational research and experimenting with different approaches to teaching, interviews faculty regarding successes and failures in the classroom and conducts regular collegewide workshops on pedagogy and the goals and missions of the college. The new faculty evaluation forum opens up the merit review process and permits a dialogue between a merit candidate and the reviewing committee (formerly a secretive body in the university) on student and peer evaluations of the candidate's teaching, the competency of his or her written evaluations of students, research progress, and the faculty member's overall contributions to Oakes. The divisional forums focus on topics for possible joint teaching efforts, and investigate common research interests that could lead to joint efforts or the sharing of information already gathered by a particular individual.

An indirect but very important aspect of our faculty development program was the creation of a strong support services program that serves the dual function of more effectively meeting students' needs and taking student pressures off the faculty. The supportive services program provides tutorial support and special instruction in writing, science and mathematics; extensive psychological counseling; a special program of administrative counseling geared to help "newcomers" to the university understand and work through the bureaucratic maze; special counseling programs on financial aid (apart from the campuswide office) and career planning. The program reduces the number of nonclassroom contact hours between faculty and students while enhancing the quality of those hours. Faculty are permitted to focus more on student problems related to their courses and academic programs. Thus both students and faculty are more adequately served. This is particularly true for women and minority faculty who are frequently called on to be models and tutors as well as teachers.

In addition to these specific activities, the college has maintained a position entitled *preceptor for faculty development*. This is a senior faculty member who has the responsibility for meeting regularly with junior faculty, in groups and individually, to discuss their plans, progress, and problems, and make recommendations to the college for adequately serving the faculty. The preceptor for faculty development also reviews all the responsibilities of each faculty member for the college, the board of studies, the academic division, the academic senate and the central administration, and mediates between all these groups to reduce the demands on each individual faculty member.

The results of this approach to faculty development at Oakes College have been impressive. Of the eleven faculty (eight ethnic) who have joined Oakes without completion of the dissertation, nine now hold the Ph.D. degree. The other two joined the faculty more recently and are making good progress toward completing their Ph.D. requirements. If these two do complete their requirements, Oakes will remain the only college on campus to have a 100 percent dissertation completion rate. Second, interdisciplinary core curricula in each of the three liberal arts disciplines have been designed. The prototype social science core course was first offered in the fall of 1975 and the majority of "spin-off" courses have already been offered at least once; the humanities core course and "spin-off" courses were offered in spring 1976. In addition, over twenty courses related to the ethnic experience in America have already been offered. Several new courses are pending academic senate approval.

A third result of the program is improved communication among the faculty. Not only is the Oakes faculty now engaged in ongoing pedagogical dialogue, but several campuswide boards of studies have used our pedagogy committee investigations to launch their own programs. The campus task force on the improvement of instruction is using the Oakes College analysis of the differing modes of faculty evaluation to generate a campuswide discussion on possible "uniform" procedures for faculty evaluation. Fourth, the program has given faculty the time, encouragement, and support they need to pursue research interests. During 1975–1976, 50 percent of the faculty were published in scholarly journals. Two have books awaiting publication decisions. And, as mentioned above, several others completed their dissertations for the Ph.D. Although the faculty development program has been reasonably successful to date—particularly in facilitating the completion of dissertations and the development of programs—Oakes is still extremely concerned with the ultimate retention (tenure) of its twenty-one junior faculty. It is these faculty—eleven of whom are ethnic and six of whom are women—with their commitments to a moral and ethical educational philosophy, basic institutional change, and the educating of a new student clientele, who can ultimately help restructure the university along more humane lines. To do so, however, requires that they reach secure positions in the institutional framework with the attendant power (particularly campuswide committee assignments) that comes with such position.

The publish-or-perish dictum is still prevalent at the University of California, and with the exceptional demands placed on Oakes College faculty we must ensure that they have sufficient time over a long time range to pursue and finish creative and scholarly academic research. To this end, the college has designed a six-year nonsabbatical leave program that would give untenured faculty members every sixth quarter off to work full-time on their research. If these leaves can be combined with summers, it will give individuals substantial, unencumbered blocs of time. The release time would not affect faculty sabbaticals, which generally come much too late to affect the tenure decision anyway.

We are convinced that with a comparatively modest investment we can inaugurate a tenure-review program that would have a tremendous impact on the University of California. It would increase tenure opportunities for a relatively large number of individuals from groups often previously "overlooked" in the university system. At the same time, we would effectively demonstrate to our faculty our support for their exceptional efforts. They would know that their commitment to equal educational opportunity and the efforts involved need not have adverse effects on their careers. We hope to initiate this program within a short period of time.

The multiracial composition of the faculty and students of Oakes College presents exciting and demanding challenges. We have worked toward an academic program that will meet the needs of the students without compromising the integrity of faculty aspirations and goals. A careful analysis of student needs and faculty goals allowed us to develop a flexible program that has sufficient variety to accomplish our purposes with a high level of success. The specific aspects of the Oakes model reflect the unique nature of the institution, but faculty development programs can be equally as successful in other institutions if accompanied by a willingness to recognize and meet the professional needs of faculty. There will be as many different faculty development programs as there are types of institutions, but all such programs can ultimately benefit students as well as faculty.

11

Financing the
Independent Sector

John R. Silber

The financing of higher education cannot ultimately be considered merely as a matter of finance. For this reason, I have been urging several imperatives for the independent sector. First, it should cease to be called—and should stop calling itself—the private sector. It consists of public institutions in the service of the public. They may be independently owned and privately supported, but all institutions of higher education, whether state-owned or independently owned, educate the public. Independent colleges and universities are private only in their sponsorship. In every other respect they are public: they are open to the public, they educate the public and nothing else but the public. By the same standard, the state-owned institutions are of course also public, but they are not the only public institutions. If we use the term *public* as a synonym for *state-owned,* we misstate the facts by implying that only an institution owned and operated by the state can be public.

By such misstatements, we mislead ourselves and also mislead the Congress, for it will ask "Why should the government subsidize the activities of private institutions with public funds?" There is no easy answer to that question as long as we wrongly label institutions. By doing so we set up an unnecessary rhetorical hurdle that must be cleared before there can be any discussion of the basic issues. It is very important, then, that we in higher education by our own usage help the public recognize that this country has only *one* system of public higher education with *two* sectors—a state-owned sector and an independently owned sector. The linguistic reform required is not extensive: it does not take very much effort to get used to it. But it is dangerously confusing to continue to act as if it were relatively unimportant.

It is also imperative to distinguish between cost and price. The distinction is fundamental. A serious mistake is made when anyone claims that the state sector has a lower cost for education than the independent sector. It is only the price that is low in the state sector. The state price is subsidized by the taxpayer and is artificially low: it may even approach the limiting condition when, as at the City University of New York, it reaches zero. But the cost is not made low just because the price is low, and we should not perpetuate this confusion.

I have also been arguing that no special group of institutions should present the case for independent higher education by suggesting that all independent institutions face a financial crisis. They do not. Twenty-two of the approximately 1,500 independent colleges and universities have 40 percent of all the endowment in the independent sector and 8.8 percent of its students. The remaining 1,420 or so have 50 percent of the endowment and 91.2 percent of the students. Harvard alone has 9 percent of the total endowment; Yale has 4 percent. What the administrators in such well-endowed schools call *problems,* we at Boston University call *solutions.*

The independent sector weakens its case by letting it be thought that all its members are in trouble, because the foundations, in order to respond to this alleged general malaise, rush to save the universities that they rightly consider irreplaceable, but that have, perhaps, the smallest need. Thus foundations have given, over the last decade, more than $150 million to only three institutions, while giving only a small fraction of this amount to more than a score of universities with high-quality programs and much greater need. This practice will continue as long as the myth that all independent universities are poor is perpetuated.

Another dangerous confusion that must be ended is a pervasive misuse of the term *subsidy*. Many in the independent sector speak of its need for a subsidy from the government if it is to continue to work. This also misstates the situation. In fact, the independent sector *subsidizes the taxpayer* nationally to the extent of at least $8 billion a year—$6 billion in operating expense and $2 billion in annualized capital expense. Eight billion dollars is a conservative estimate but even so it represents a very substantial subsidy of the taxpayer. If a national program were to reduce the current subsidy provided by the independent sector by granting $2 billion in student aid to those enrolled in the independent sector, this grant would compensate the independent sector for its public services at no more than $.25 on the dollar. At current levels, the independent sector is the golden goose that provides a dollar's worth of egg for every $.06 of federal and state ration. The goose, of course, is slowly starving on that ration and will eventually cease to lay eggs; on a modestly improved ration of $.30, it would continue to subsidize the taxpayer by laying golden eggs. The independent sector should be asking compensation for the subsidy it makes to the public weal. There can be no such thing as a subsidy for the independent sector until the federal and state governments provide more than $8 billion annually to it. No one foresees that day.

It is in the interest of both sectors of public higher education, and of society as well, that the independent sector continue to provide its subsidy to the taxpayer. There is no reason in principle why the state governments should not now begin to extend to students in the independent sector the entitlement they already extend to students in the state sector. There is no plausible reason for the existing discriminatory pattern, because the slanderous charge that the independent sector is a haven for the indolent rich is refuted by the facts. The Census Bureau has recently reported that while 53 percent of the students in the state sector come from families with incomes less than $15,000, the figure for the independent sector is fully 41 percent.

As a matter of practical finance, few of the states are now able to extend this entitlement to students in the independent sector. That is, most states are heavily dependent on the subsidy from the independent sector. If substantial new support is to come for the independent sector, it almost certainly must come from the federal government.

This is not a time, unfortunately, when higher education has the sort of prestige and public support that makes lobbying for massive funding an easy task. If the independent sector is to be supported through federal legislation, it will be necessary not only to free ourselves and Congress of the confusions I have discussed, but also to ensure that higher education as we practice it is worthy and is seen to be worthy of federal support.

A considerable part of the argument for any tax support of higher education is based on its education and certification of competent persons to do the world's work. In our justifiable concern that no qualified student be denied the opportunity to study for and achieve certification, we must take great care not to subvert and eventually destroy the value of the certification.

The interests of society and of the individual alike require that each citizen of the United States be educated to the limit of his ability. Whenever a qualified student is unable to attend college because he or his parents cannot afford to pay, there is a denial of equal opportunity as well as a waste of human potential. All education must continue to be dedicated to removing ethnic, racial, and economic barriers that stand between qualified students and their educational fulfillment. I believe this as a citizen and as an educator.

Some maintain that financial barriers ought to be lowered only in the state-controlled sector of public higher education. They support large tax subsidies to state institutions so that the tuition price is low. At the same time, they oppose state subsidies to students attending independent colleges and universities. The poor, they insist, ought to be educated in state institutions or not at all. In contrast, I believe that the state ought to subsidize the education of qualified students rather than any particular institutions. Any qualified, economically deprived student should be able to take advantage of the full range of choice available in our system of higher education.

Racial or economic barriers to achieving higher education are essentially manmade and therefore to a large extent
man can remove them. But there is an insurmountable barrier
to higher education that man cannot remove. If someone lacks
aptitude for higher education, he will never achieve it, no matter how strenuously his society may work to make it available
to him. Society cannot educate a person without aptitude; all it
can do is to create a redundant place in college for him, engage
redundant faculty to fail in teaching him, and finally award him
a fraudulent diploma. It is superfluous to say that someone
without aptitude should be denied access to higher education.
A person without aptitude will be denied meaningful access
by his own inability.

There are certainly students with the basic intellectual
endowment necessary for higher education who have been so
fearfully neglected in the lower schools that their potential to
be college freshmen has been seriously damaged. For these
students, the answer is clearly not open (but essentially meaningless) admission to institutions of higher education followed
by automatic (and therefore also meaningless) graduation, but
remedial programs that will develop their abilities so that they
can profit from higher education. But such programs, which
could be offered at community colleges, should not be confused
with higher education. Such programs are a necessary *precondi-
tion* to higher education. They are also preferable, educationally
and morally, to the shabby confidence game whereby students
who have not attained eighth-grade levels in reading or mathematics are run through the revolving door of "open admissions."

Limiting higher education to those with aptitude would
not limit access to higher education to some sort of social elite,
excluding large numbers of people simply because they wish to
follow trades rather than professions. It is patent snobbery to
suggest that the aptitude for higher education is any less common among carpenters or janitors than among college presidents. Not only do I have no objection to the idea of educated
carpenters and janitors—I believe that carpenters and janitors
with the aptitude for higher education ought to get it.

But it is highly misleading to claim that everyone can be
equally educated by four years of college. It is plain folly to say
that anyone can learn to do anything. It is a sign of the extent
to which standards have been abandoned that I need to point

out that not everyone has the ability to be a surgeon or an air traffic controller, no matter which course of study he is exposed to. Everyone realizes that a blind man cannot become a painter, or a paraplegic a football player. It is only a little less apparent that the palsied cannot practice brain surgery. Neither should those of feeble memory pursue the law nor those without hearing be trained to conduct orchestras. I am not suggesting that people cannot or should not perform at the limits of their ability. But no one can transcend his actual limitations. An educational system that encourages futile attempts at impossible transcendence is at best a cruel deception. At worst, it is a racket.

The claim that everyone has equal ability is still more pernicious when it says that anyone can gain a credential for any job he wants. There is an obvious societal interest in ensuring that certain crucial occupations will be practiced only by the competent. That is why credentials were established to begin with. No one wants to be operated on by a surgeon who got his license as a gift, or defended by a lawyer who bought his admission to the bar. Every time we go up in an airplane, it becomes a matter of life and death to us that the credentials given air traffic controllers be entirely honest ones.

It is just another cruel deception when institutions suggest that all credentials (even deserved ones) can be honored. Our economy does not automatically create jobs just because we award credentials for them. There is striking evidence of this in a recent report that 17.2 percent of new Ph.D.s in chemistry had no prospect of employment when they attained their degrees.[1] For Ph.D.s in English, the figure was 21.5 percent. This is a harsh present, but the future will be harsher still: the Bureau of Labor Statistics estimates that between 1972 and 1985, a total of 583,000 new Ph.D.s will compete for 187,000 jobs. That is, two out of three of these professionals will never practice the professions for which, at great societal and personal investment, they have been trained. If they have pursued their graduate study purely as training for a union card, with no thought of personal fulfillment, they will regard a significant portion of their life as a foolish waste. The more fortunate

[1]Gene I. Maeroff, "Teaching Job Prospects for Graduates with Doctorates Reported to Be Growing Worse," *The New York Times,* January 21, 1976: 27.

among them will attain happy lives as cultivated individuals. Others will lead embittered lives.

When students are encouraged to prepare for jobs they will never hold, a serious question of ethics arises. This is usually recognized when fly-by-night vocational schools encourage students to train for nonexistent jobs, but ethics are no less relevant when respectable universities prepare college teachers who will be lucky to find employment in which their skills will be even marginally useful.

This ethical problem does not arise when education is treated as education rather than as training, where opportunities for training are not mindlessly expanded beyond foreseeable need, and where there are reasonable standards for admission to higher education and graduation from it. But society's obligation to provide higher education ought to be limited to those who have some aptitude and who want to become educated. The educational fulfillment of all qualified citizens, allowing them to become educated to the highest level of which they are capable, presents our system of higher education with sufficient challenge.

Water in a milk carton is still water. We cannot offer higher education by contradicting the very concept through mindlessly egalitarian certification that ignores competence. When we do, we deny the purpose and destroy the value of an education. If we continue in this direction—mocking the value of a genuine education by treating certification, however fraudulent, as its only purpose—we should not be surprised if Congress is unwilling to fund higher education. Congressional impatience with the adulteration of education will be directed evenly at both state and independent sectors of higher education, for in these practices both sectors fail to meet the criterion of public service.

The public should not, will not, and ultimately cannot tolerate the practice of equating equal opportunity with equal achievement. But the large majority of high-minded citizens who care about the achievement of constitutional objectives can be persuaded to support practices that will give full meaning and substance to the concept of equal opportunity and to the principle of choice in the selection of one's educational institution.

The most appropriate form for federal aid to higher education is not institutional aid but student aid. Awarding aid to students makes clear in form what is true in substance—that the beneficiaries of tax support for higher education are not the institutions but rather their students. The free choice of students, acting in a relatively free market, is a better means for channeling aid than any legislative or bureaucratic process for identifying deserving institutions.

In this connection, I believe that we should discourage dependency on loans for the financing of undergraduate education. It is entirely appropriate that every graduate of a medical school should pay back $40,000 or so of the cost of his education as a small levy against his very large income. As long as we expect taxi owners to pay $30,000 (about two years' salary) for a license, we can expect physicians to pay $40,000 (which is less than one year's average income) for their training. But it can be disastrous for a graduate from a poor family to leave school with a debt of $5,000. If such a graduate marries a spouse with a similar debt, the couple have a combined negative dowry of $10,000. They will be lucky to own a house. If they have themselves come to college out of poverty, they will be prevented from escaping it. At best they will be stranded on its margin and at worst return to its center.

From the point of view of Congress, people whose $10,000 negative dowry prevents them from buying a house are a serious problem: they depress the housing industry. Presented to the Congress seriously and effectively, this argument can carry a good deal of weight.

What is needed is a reformation of the present federal student aid program. The half cost restricted on the Basic Equal Opportunity Grant should remain, and its maximum value should be increased to $1,600. And a measure of self-help should be introduced in the requirements for a Supplementary Equal Opportunity Grant (SEOG). It would be entirely reasonable to require $1,000 of self-help before a student is eligible for an SEO grant. A student who is not willing to work nine hours a week at the minimum wage does not have sufficient motivation for higher education to justify public support in gaining it.

The requirement of $1,000 of self-help for an SEOG would shift the distribution of SEOG funds from the present

70/30 ratio favoring the state sector to 70/30 ratio favoring the independent sector. This shift would substantially narrow the tuition gap and thereby give more students the opportunity to choose between state and independent institutions. Although this change in the distribution of SEOG funds appears to favor the independent sector, the total package still distributes the majority of funds to students in the state sector, for the present allocation of SEOG funds favors students in the state sector by a ratio of 70/30. Such a redistribution would assign to each of the major components in the federal package a well-defined role. The SEOG would serve to guarantee access, ensuring (along with the state subsidy now granted to the state sector) that no qualified student would be denied higher education merely because he could not pay for it.

The SEOG (aided by a measure of required self-help) would assure each qualified student the full range of choice offered by our highly diversified system of public higher education. As long as public policy dictates that access be offered the economically deprived student only in state institutions, expanding the range of choice will require an increasingly wasteful duplication of resources. All the demographic data tell us that we are already seriously overbuilt; further development in the state sector can only exacerbate a dangerous situation.

Increased federal aid now appears the only hope for substantial and generally available new support for the independent sector. But increased federal aid alone cannot save the independent sector. It seems clear now that an independent institution, in order to survive the coming shake-out, will need to develop its own resources and learn to manage them with great care. The continuing decline in births has already assured that the admissions pool will shrink each year after 1978, and, we can expect approximately 4.5 million fewer persons between the ages of eighteen and twenty-four by the year 2000. Even if we were to raise the proportion of high school graduates attending college—that is, to exaggerate the tendencies that have already transformed the meaning of higher education—we should be dealing with a catastrophic decline in enrollments. It is mathematically possible that we could offset this decline by extraordinary increases in continuing education enrollments—say 16 million new part-time students—but there is no reason to assume that we will, and it would be suicidal to plan on the basis of such a forlorn hope.

We will be far wiser to seek ways to make use of an increasingly large surplus capacity. One promising possibility is leasing unused facilities to universities in the developing world, which would be enabled to conduct their own programs of education through programs of instruction that they themselves have developed. Their students can experience the benefits and challenges of living in a complex technological society that foreshadows the direction of development of their native countries. Such overseas programs of education could be developed without spending a cent of precious capital on facilities, and the cost of the lease could be met through barter agreements negotiated between the United States and the developing countries. The nations of the developing world can learn from the sad experience of the United States taxpayer just how expensive redundant brick and mortar can be. The universities of the United States have long gained invaluable educational advantages from their overseas operations. It is time for us to return the favor, and in so doing recoup some of the losses of redundancy.

It is essential that we not treat the problems of funding independent higher education in isolation. We must realize that there are two sectors in one national system of higher education. The independent sector has recently founded a new organization, the National Association of Independent Colleges and Universities (NAICU). This group will have as its primary purpose articulating and advocating a legislative position for the independent sector. But it would be a mistake for the state sector to regard NAICU as a hostile entity. This association will give the independent sector, for the first time, an organization that can address the various associations of state colleges and universities and that can work to develop positions that express the common interest of all higher education.

It is inevitable that when the interests of the two sectors are in opposition—something that happens less frequently than is commonly believed—there will be compromises. It is better for higher education that these compromises, as far as possible, be worked out, not in the legislative arena by the politicians, but within higher education itself.

If higher education can arrange these compromises within its own community, then it can approach Congress with a single purpose and a single voice. The two sectors will be fighting side by side rather than against each other. The needs of society and these constituencies demand no less.

The two sectors of our system of public higher education share equally in a future freighted with risk. They share also the challenge and bright promise of educating a nation. Their partnership is inevitable; the question is whether they will be able to carry it on successfully. The best hope that they will lies in a path of mutual respect and rationally determined compromise. Once they understand this, the risks will no longer daunt them and they can set themselves to fulfilling the promise.

12

Institutional versus Student Aid

George B. Weathersby

The choice between different forms of student assistance and institutional assistance to support postsecondary
education is a lively topic these days. There are a number of
reasons for the recent increase in discussion and concern about
this choice. First, state support of postsecondary education has
expanded in the last four or five years much more rapidly in
the student aid sector than in the institutional sector. Second,
there is a real difference between federal financing and state
financing. The major thrust of the federal role is student assistance. Direct federal institutional assistance programs are very
small compared to federal student assistance programs. On the
other hand, the state support for postsecondary institutions
is primarily in the form of institutional assistance. The differences between federal and state roles have to be articulated and
coordinated in some way. We need to understand those articu-
lations and interrelationships much better than we now do.

A third reason why the institutional-student support choice is important involves the whole debate about public policy toward the state and independent sectors. If accessibility to public funds is determined by the type of institution, it will probably mean the end of the independent sector in most states. If students are the basic, initial receivers of public assistance, then the independent and the proprietary sectors will share indirectly in public support. Quite simply, institutional survival is at stake. The decline in the eighteen- to twenty-four-year-old population will be about 25 percent from 1980 to 1985. Whether institutions survive or die will depend a great deal on the amount of money they have; whether that money is directed through student or institutional channels will have a great deal to do with not only how many but also with which institutions survive.

A final reason for the concern about institutional and student financing is that in a very pragmatic sense postsecondary education now has low priority in a number of states and among the general public. The financial crisis now prevalent at state and institutional levels suggests that the amount of additional support for postsecondary education for the future is likely to be small, particularly relative to our expectations.

With this background let me suggest some basic concepts that underlie choices between institutional and student assistance. First, for a number of reasons individuals seek postsecondary education. For a number of quite different reasons, postsecondary educational institutions are willing to admit applicants. It is not so much a marketplace as a marriage brokerage. Student admission and resource allocation decisions are not made by the market mechanism but by an untidy process of people seeking sets of social, intellectual, personal, and interpersonal environments. The choice that an individual makes is much more informed by the past than it is by the present or by predictions for the future. A concern for the job market, for what the future will be like is much less a factor than the role of alumni, the previous reputation of a campus, the campus environment, or whether it has a winning football team.

Let me examine some assumptions commonly made about student aid and institutional aid as the basic means of financial intervention. First, it is generally argued that student assistance is intended to do three things: increase access to postsecondary education, increase choice among various forms of postsecondary education and, some would add, redistribute income. For the first objective, the evidence is that there is a very weak relationship between the net price a student pays and the likelihood of attending a particular institution.[1] The basic assumption is that a large proportion of individuals would go to college if it were not for the price they have to pay. This assumption just is not true. An examination of individuals with different incomes facing different prices indicates that the effect of price is quite small. A more realistic view is that price subsidies can be used to increase access to postsecondary education, but the cost to the funder will be something like $3,000 to $5,000 for each additional student added to enrollment.

The next assumption is that student aid will provide greater choice among the various institutional forms. According to this viewpoint, as the price of one sector changes—for example, a lowered price in the independent sector relative to the state sector—people will switch from the public to the private sector, though not at a rapid rate. I have already noted the low responsiveness to price within a sector, by which it costs about $4,000 for each student added to enrollment. Between sectors, the change is even less. It costs about ten times more, or $40,000, to create incentives for one student to switch sectors. In other words, the realistic expectation we should have of the consequences of price equalization is that the distribution of students among sectors will remain about the same. This seems to go against basic logic because the implicit assumption is that everybody would go to the same institution if somehow they could all get in academically and if they could afford the price. But this assumption denies the fact that basic preferences for postsecondary education are a combination of many factors that go beyond the simple perception of what is a good school or a bad school, what is an expensive or an inexpensive one. Determining factors have to do with social environment, peer groups, parents, communities, and future expectations. Obviously, public policy does not propose to change all of these fac-

[1] See G. A. Jackson and G. B. Weathersby, "Individual Demand for Higher Education, *Journal of Higher Education 46* (1975):

tors. Therefore, if these factors stay constant and if just the price of attendance changes, there will be very little change in the demand among sectors. This point should be kept in mind when the use of increased student assistance to increase student access and choice is considered.

The third intention of student assistance is redistributing income. Currently about 24 percent of the eighteen- to twenty-four-year-olds attend postsecondary institutions; it is an area that does not involve most young Americans. Education past high school is the first time past the age of six when there is a minority of the age cohort participating in education. Therefore, it is an unlikely point at which to intervene to redistribute income. With continuing high unemployment, the parents of college students should probably have low priority as beneficiaries of income redistribution.

On another level, we make the following assumptions about how individuals choose schools: first, we assume that the existence of student assistance programs means students have information about the programs; second, we assume that if students have this information, it will change their decisions about where or if they go to school. To test the first part of this logic, a student of mine did something very simple. She wrote a letter to the financial aid office in every school in the city of Boston asking them what it costs to attend their school. In her letter she indicated that she was a twenty-two-year-old woman who had been working as a clerk for the last four years. She said she was self-supporting but had not saved much money, would like to continue school, and would like to know what the net price would be, including likely student assistance. It seemed like a nice, straightforward question. To determine how many post-secondary education institutions there were in Boston we called the Department of Health, Education and Welfare, which sent us a list of seventy-seven institutions approved for basic grants and/or guaranteed student loans. On investigation, it turned out that sixty-eight of them exist; nine do not. I do not know if that is a normal error or whether Boston is unique in having phantom institutions.

Of the sixty-eight schools that existed, two thirds answered the letter; one third did not. Only one of the public institutions answered. Of the two thirds that answered, only half of them (or one third) admitted that they had any federally sponsored financial aid programs. Yet the sample list was entirely composed of institutions eligible for basic grants and/or guaranteed student loans. Only one tenth, or five institutions, included the forms for basic grants in their response and none of them included any information on the average awards. All of the schools encouraged students to contact the financial aid officer, which is what this student had in fact done with her first letter. In other words, it is impossible in the city of Boston to find out the net price of attending postsecondary education by simply asking. It turns out that if you apply, are admitted, and pay your tuition deposits, schools will send you notification of your financial aid award. At an average cost of application and tuition deposit of $100 per institution, that works out to $6,800 as the price, in the city of Boston, for information on the net cost of attending college. This happens to be about twice the annual total cost to the student of attending any of these institutions.

The point of this example is that the first step of the logic is absolutely false. Potential students *cannot* obtain the information—the net price of attending a particular institution—that could potentially affect their decisions. And even if they could obtain it, there is not much evidence that knowing the price in fact affects the decision. The effect of price information depends on when in the application, admissions, and decision process the information becomes available. By April 1, an individual may have applied to three places, been admitted to two, and be trying to decide which one to attend. At this point, the magnitude and composition of financial aid might not make any difference. The strength of the relationship between finance and an individual's choice of college strikes me as much less than what policymakers generally assume.

The other major policy alternative is to consider increasing the support to institutions. Howard Bowen's formula is pretty candid: schools raise all the money they can, spend all they raise, and make internal allocation decisions according to internal and external politics. This is a brief and oversimplified summary of how colleges finance themselves—but let us examine what is assumed in that chain of causality. First, we assume that an increase in public subsidy implies an increase in total income available to the institution. Second, we assume that increasing the total income leads to increased total expenditures. Third, we assume that increased total expenditures indicate increases in the quality or quantity of educational outcomes.

These assumptions leave room for many questions. First, is there any evidence that an increase in the amount of public subsidy increases the total institutional income? In the public sector, to which the largest institutional subsidies go, the subsidy provided to an institution is viewed by most states as a substitute for an amount that would otherwise be charged to students. In most states, the tuition rate is determined by taking the total of approved expenditures, subtracting the proposed state appropriation, and dividing by the estimated number of students. In this way, what is affected by the public allocation is not the total budget of an institution but the share of the total cost that the students bear. Therefore, changes in the level of state appropriation do not necessarily result in changes in the total expenditure level but may result in changes in who pays for the given total expenditure level. By contrast, in private or independent institutions, which have a variety of income sources, some of which are quite responsive, the effect of such funds may be very real. But if institutional support is viewed solely as a substitute for other funds, it will probably have little impact.

I recently spent some time at an elite private men's college that currently has 800 students and is proposing an expansion to 1,000 students for financial reasons. As I looked over their budget, I noticed one glaring deficit account: the student aid account had a total income of $37,000 and a total expenditure of $717,000, while the entire institution was running a $250,000 deficit. School officials said that they required all of their students to apply for basic grants and that 41 out of 800 had received them that year. In addition they awarded grants to 300 students, or an average of $2,200 to almost half of the student body. The college administrators said they were worried that they might not get as many students as they would like and had been increasing the awards up to the point where they were now just about breaking the school. If I understand their logic, they are proposing to increase enrollments to 1,000 so that they can cover their deficit by increasing student aid. The point is that having what appears to be more income does not necessarily mean that there is more income in aggregate. The amount they were discounting in grants was as much as the net profit they were getting.

The second assumption about institutional aid is that increasing income would increase total expenditures. However, after looking at the debt overhang in colleges today and the rate of increase of that debt, particularly from insured borrowing, it is apparent that institutions are spending a lot more than they are earning. Given this tendency to spend more than one has, it is likely that increasing the income of colleges by public subsidy would simply increase the amount of expenditures over that income. I think the ability to spend less than revenues, a relationship that really has not been explained in most of the discussions about finance, will probably be the key factor in determining which institutions survive and which fail.

The third assumption involves the relationship between expenditure and outcome. We usually assume that an institution that has more money and spends more money must do more good things, educate more students, improve the quality of that education. But we have some startling evidence that institutions with similar technology, dealing with similar students in a similar environment, vary in the amount of resources that they use by as much as six to one. For example, some institutions average a cost per student of $900, while similar institutions with similar relative quality average $5,900.[2] If one compares the efficient institutions to the average ones in a particular sector (four-year liberal arts colleges, for example) one finds that the average institution could either spend about 30 percent less or increase the number of students and the amount of service it provides by about 30 percent. In other words, the amount of investment in quality of life or in faculty preference or in whatever this additional 30 percent is currently going to is absolutely enormous. Such differences among institutions certainly raise the question of whether we are dealing with a very efficient sector.

Another facet of the operational structure of institutions is shown in a very interesting model of "prestige-maximizing"

[2]D. Breneman, "An Economic Theory of Ph.D. Production," Ford Foundation Research Program in University Administration (University of California, Berkeley, 1970).

behavior put together by a Senior Fellow at the Brookings Institution. Whether a school is technical, vocational, graduate,
or undergraduate, one of the major concerns about the quality
of a department is the placement record of graduates. If recent
graduates go to places that are viewed to be attractive—that is,
to good jobs, good institutions, or good locations—then their
departments gain in prestige. Prestige is judged essentially by
two characteristics: first, where graduates go, what they do, and
what their characteristics are; and second, some assessment of
the quality of the program and the faculty of a particular department. The kind and quality of jobs available to students is a
function of at least two things. One is the market—the number
of jobs that are opening up on an annual basis—and an institution cannot control the market very much. The other is the degree of competition relative to the market—how many other
schools are training people in very similar ways. Each institution wants to regulate its output so that it does not flood the
market or have too many graduates relative to the number of
high-prestige jobs available. Otherwise, graduates will be taking
less-than-prestigious placements that cause acute embarrassment in the academic world. In terms of input, there are incentives to increase the number of students enrolled because that
is how one generates more revenue, more faculty, and more diverse course offerings. With larger enrollments one can probably differentiate beginning and advance levels, generate some
people who are talented as teaching fellows, get a bigger share
of the resource pie on campus and, thereby, increase political
influence. Thus, there are many reasons for maximizing the
quantity of resources that one can control independent of the
decisions made about who goes out.

My favorite example of this prestige-maximizing model
is the philosophy department of the University of California at
Berkeley, consistently rated by the American Council on Education (ACE) as one of the very best departments of philosophy
in the country. For twenty-two consecutive years this department graduated three Ph.D.s annually. These people all went
on to one of five or six institutions, including Harvard, Princeton, Yale, and Chicago. During these twenty-two years, enrollment rose from fifteen to as much as sixty-five or seventy, though
it has now come down a little. What are all those people doing?

Well, they are ensuring that we have more faculty, that we have teaching fellows to teach undergraduate courses, that we have people to take advanced seminars in philosophy, and that we have ways of justifying numerous differentiations of philosophy. However, the department is very careful not to graduate more than three of these people a year because that is all who can be placed in prestigious jobs. I am not saying that every school fits this model but Berkeley does illustrate what appears to be inordinately inefficient behavior by departments, albeit behavior that is highly consistent with their notion of prestige maximization.

I have invented another paradigm that I call *family maximizing behavior,* which is the extreme opposite of prestige maximization. The purpose of this behavior, which might be found in a small liberal arts college, is to build a closely knit departmental family. For this model you need just enough faculty to cover the basic areas, but not too many, because then they will fight with each other, form cliques, and challenge your authority as an administrator. At the same time, you want to have the minimum number of students. You have to have some students because they pay for the school but if you let in too many the school becomes impersonal and not supportive. Such institutions have some of the same problems as a family. There is the problem of aging that tenured faculty are starting to experience, and euthanasia, also called *early retirement,* is a popular topic these days. There is the problem of family therapy; we call that *faculty development.* There is the problem of family counseling; we call that *faculty evaluation.* There is the problem of public welfare, in which some families receive public subsidy; we call that *financing private institutions.*

These examples of departmental behavior are meant to illustrate some of the different ways of using resources. I have mentioned them in some detail because it is only within the limits of a particular model of behavior that one can forecast what changes in the level of resources would have an impact on activities and outcomes.

This discussion suggests three ways of looking at the alternatives of institutional and student support: from the standpoints of effectiveness, efficiency, and equity. First, how effective are different alternatives in accomplishing different objectives?

Students, faculty, administrators, staff, members of boards of trustees, state and federal government officers, executive and legislative officials, and association officers all have their own sets of objectives and some financing methods are very effective for one objective and not for others. Most of the objectives cannot be measured in ways that are acceptable to all concerned and, therefore, there may be no agreement on how well a particular objective was met. One's notion of what objectives are and how they can be measured is critical for evaluating effectiveness.

Some obvious conclusions about funding can be drawn when it is viewed from the standpoint of effectiveness. One is that bloc grants—unrestricted grants to any participant—should only be given when the sponsor believes that the recipient's objectives match his own and when virtually all participants in an institution share those same objectives. Another conclusion is that, if one believes that the recipient shares the same values or objectives as the funder, decision making on some issues can be decentralized. To effectively decentralize, one has to show that the people who are making the decisions as recipients share the same notions of effectiveness, the same objectives, and the same agreed-to measures.

A second standpoint is efficiency. Efficient financing of colleges and universities requires focusing funds at the margin. Marginal funding is a fundamental principle to understand. Suppose one funds a group of people 95 percent of whom would have gone to college anyway and 5 percent of whom would have been encouraged to attend as a result of financial aid. To pay for the 100 percent in order to have an effect on the 5 percent means that 95 percent of what is paid for is decisons that would have been made the same way anyway. Marginal funding of students would require identifying which 5 of the 100 actually were additional enrollees. You cannot look at a group of people and sort out who would have gone and would not have gone. There is just no way of telling when everyone applies at about the same time of year for basic grants that 95 percent of the applicants would be going anyway.

On the other hand, marginal funding is possible at the institutional level because instead of identifying particular people, one can identify the changes in aggregate quantities. Consequently, one of the reasons a funder might want to consider funding institutions in proportion to changes in characteristics is the inherent efficiency of that approach. For example, if a school has 100 people of a particular category (such as low-income students or state residents) enrolled this year, and next year the enrollment rises to 125, there is a marginal increase of 25 students. They cannot be identified by name, but one can determine that the institution has an increase of 25 in the category of interest. The institution would be funded at a fixed amount per incremental student, and funders would control their actual marginal cost.

It is very difficult to compare the efficiency of different financing systems. One can estimate the efficiency of student assistance in terms of access, and that is costing $4,000 or $5,000 per additional student. The cost per additional student of institutional support is impossible to estimate because it depends on what the institution does with the money. However, by funding changes in characteristics one can control directly the marginal cost, the cost per additional student. Funders must decide as a matter of policy whether to choose strategies that enable them to control the marginal cost of the funding decision or strategies that enable them to control the average cost of the funding decision, such as basic grants.

A third standpoint is equity. I believe public policymakers think of equity in terms of means rather than ends, in terms of who gets the check rather than what are the consequences of funding. Using the means of funding as the main criterion for judging equity, subsidized tuition is by far the most equitable basis of distributing money. Every person who takes part in postsecondary education would get a subsidy in tuition in the public and private sectors. There would be no differentiation or discrimination at all. On the other hand, this strategy is not very efficient. A strategy that appears slightly less equitable would be to provide student assistance that discriminates in some way, in terms of income, in terms of ability, or by sectors. Such a strategy is more targeted and therefore less equitable. A third strategy would be various kinds of institutional support, which tends in some ways to be least equitable of all. On the other hand, if the objective is to be equitable in terms of ends rather than means, the order of equity among strategies would reverse, because there are ways of funding institutions that deal with marginal categories that would be far more equitable than alternative ways of funding students.

Thus I come to the conclusion people have come to expect from an academic these days: we are dealing with a very complicated problem for which there is no universal answer. There is no system of financing that is uniformly effective, efficient, and equitable. It depends very much on one's objectives and one's assumptions about how people and institutions behave.

13

The Case for Selective Entitlement Vouchers

George J. Nolfi

Adults are returning to education in ever-increasing numbers to improve or redirect their careers or simply to learn something new. In the last decade the proportion of adults participating in some type of classroom education has increased from one in thirteen to one in eight. Most enroll in only one or two courses at a time and regard study as secondary to other activities, such as family and work. This learning scene has been labeled *adult education, lifelong learning, continuing education,* and—the term used here—*recurrent education.*

This chapter draws heavily on several studies the author has performed at the request of the Commonwealth of Massachusetts, and on investigations conducted under a Ford Foundation Study Grant. Papers and publications resulting from that work are cited as references. Support is gratefully acknowledged.

Recurrent education settings vary considerably. They include (with approximate percentage of total enrollments) colleges and universities (25 percent); proprietary schools (28 percent); programs sponsored by employers, unions, and the military (27 percent); community agency classes (13 percent); and countless learning opportunities sponsored by private, nonprofit organizations. This diversity of programs responds to a wide range of career and other interests of adults during the evening or on weekends, in downtown or branch campuses, and in learning formats suitable for adults who have become unfamiliar with school. Part-time study and responsiveness to consumers characterize this array of activities. This mix of activities and providers constitutes an enormous recurrent education system serving more part-time adult students than the total full-time youthful population of colleges and universities.

Recurrent education draws strength from its relative freedom from public subsidy, intervention, and control. It has been financed through private payments from users and employers and has grown in direct response to their needs. Direct accountability to users has compelled recurrent education providers to design diverse and innovative programs to meet consumer needs. The system has escaped both rigid traditions and the legislative budget process, which tend to stifle innovation and diversity.

However, there are now several compelling reasons for new public investment and policy in recurrent education. Not all adults are equally well served by the existing system. Those who benefit the most from recurrent education are adults who enjoyed the greatest educational benefits as youth. The typical adult learner is under forty, relatively affluent, internally motivated, employed as a professional or manager, and well educated (college experience or degree). This person expects a salary increase to result from his investment in recurrent education. About 75 percent of evening and continuing education students in colleges and universities say they study for job-related reasons. In contrast, many adults of low income, education, and job status are not served well by existing institutions. They often are deterred from study by financial barriers and perceptions of inevitable failure in traditional educational settings. In Massachusetts, for example, fully 25 percent of the potential prime market for expanded adult learning opportunities (adults who are both interested and willing, but often unable to pay) consists of adults with less than a high school diploma. Seventy-four percent of the skilled workers express an interest in recurrent education compared to 91 percent of the professional workers. Although both groups show high interest, actual participation rates vary dramatically.[1] This pattern probably holds true in other states with relatively minor variations.

Subsidies for those on the bottom of the economic ladder can be justified both on humanitarian and economic grounds. Billions of dollars are spent each year in welfare and unemployment payments to deal with the effects of social and economic dependency. Relatively little is spent to help the disadvantaged, the unskilled, and the chronically unemployed to develop skills by which they could improve themselves. Many skilled jobs go begging amid high unemployment because many jobseekers lack marketable skills and knowledge. Some of the personal income subsidies might be spent better for financial aid and improved information and counseling services to help disadvantaged adults match educational opportunities to realistic job and career opportunities. Helping the socially and economically depressed and improving the manpower and skills base in the economy are national concerns that justify a major investment in recurrent education. That investment could remove from the welfare rolls, and restore dignity to, many adults who have a strong desire to learn but who face barriers of cost, information, and access.

These "second-chance" and "disadvantaged" clienteles who are not being served now would study if educational services were related to the real problems of their work, their careers, and their family situations.[2] "Second-chance" clienteles are the working men and women who lack a college education,

[1]G. J. Nolfi and V. I. Nelson, *Strengthening the Alternative Postsecondary Education System: Continuing and Part-Time Study in Massachusetts.* Vol. 1. *Summary Report and Recommendation* (Cambridge, Mass.: University Consultants, 1973), 60–63.

[2]G. J. Nolfi and V. I. Nelson, *The Implementation and Operation of a State Based Adult Recurrent Education Entitlement Voucher Program to Finance Open Learning and Continuing Education* (Cambridge, Mass.: University Consultants, working paper, July 1974).

but who probably would have gone to college if they had been born twenty years later. In the course of their careers and work they have developed many postsecondary level competencies. They may hold supervisory positions, but often lose out in competition for promotions with young, recent college graduates. This displacement occurs despite the claim of personnel managers that they prefer to give middle-level management positions to experienced men and women. Investment in further education for this group would be quite cost effective socially. The "disadvantaged" clientele is characterized by low income, ethnic factors, chronic unemployment, and a number of educational deficiencies or special needs. Many are high school dropouts. Socially, this is a high priority group for public investment. The supplementary services needed to serve the disadvantaged will be expensive.

A labor leader testifying in favor of Adult Recurrent Education Entitlement Voucher legislation in Massachusetts eloquently stated the case for these groups: "The need is for programs which will hold out hope for those who in earlier years had no direction and no goals, and merely drifted along until one day they realized a short, brief period in their lives had shaped their destiny forever. These are the people that need the hope that a second chance can give them. One of the great tragedies of human existence is the despair of those who feel locked into a life of futility, who have the will to struggle, but who lack the means to struggle effectively."[3]

Training these currently unserved clienteles will meet the needs for new skills in the labor market that historically have been filled by young people coming out of school.[4] Dramatic changes are evident in the structure of this labor market as the pool of new entrants shrinks. New skill needs must be met by training those already in the labor market or ·by reaching out to those with the least skill, the least previous education, and the least access to information about how to use the educational system to their advantage.

[3]W. Ryan, oral testimony before the Joint Education Committee of the Massachusetts Legislature, Boston, Mass., April 1975.
[4]S. Dresch, "Educational Saturation: A Demographic-Economic Model," *AAUP Bulletin* (Autumn 1975).

Any subsidy program raises the question of who would receive government support and who should not. In the case of recurrent education, the nature of the existing system, of the unserved clientele, and of the current economic situation argue for a highly selective subsidy program. A subsidy that focuses on the second-chance and disadvantaged clientele both husbands tax dollars and plays to the strength of the existing system.

Any program design involves decisions about four critical policy trade-offs: (1) either more students are assisted on a part-time basis or fewer students are assisted to pursue full-time study while receiving income stipends; (2) resources are either diffused through a universal subsidy or are used in a focused way for selective subsidies to target clienteles for whom there is a high social rate of return from participation in recurrent education; (3) awards either result in the replacement of private monies now flowing into the support of recurrent education with public funds or they are used in a manner that complements those private monies and indeed stimulates further private investment in recurrent education; and (4) either the funds are diffused for a totally discretionary broad range of general interest education and activities and occupationally related education, or they are targeted first at providing necessary support for target clienteles to use additional education as a vehicle for advancement of their socioeconomic and employment positions.[5]

Since most adults prefer to study part-time, it does not make sense to provide them with a full-time subsidy. In addition, there is no need to subsidize those adults who can pay their own way or who are subsidized by employers. The real need is for a targeted approach for those who have been deterred by the cost of tuition. Proposals for a universal entitlement or educational leave do not provide this focused approach and tend to substitute public money for private investment, an effect that should be avoided.

[5]G. J. Nolfi, *Setting and Criteria for the Design of an Effective Public Policy of Educational Entitlements,* paper presented to the Seminar of Entitlements, Office of the Assistant Secretary of Education, Washington, D.C., July 1975.

Other proposals argue for direct aid to educational institutions in a fashion similar to aid for full-time higher education. While low tuition in public institutions may encourage more low income students to enroll, it also subsidizes those who would have paid on their own. In addition to being expensive, blanket subsidies to institutions would mute the competitive and innovative spirit that now exists within American recurrent education. A subsidy program should encourage the natural market character of this system that has responded so well to adults who could afford to pay.

Public policy should deal first with those problems that have the greatest social priority and that are manageable in their dimensions. Hence, policy should be aimed at expanding educational opportunity, not at reforming higher education. Much discussion of educational entitlements confuses these objectives. Differential access to recurrent education is a manageable problem that can be isolated and treated with a specific solution. Finally, a state or federal program of educational entitlements should be simple to administer. Red tape and bureaucratic regulations should be kept to a minimum.

Based on the foregoing policy considerations, a sound public policy in recurrent education would be comprised of four components: a subsidy for those who need it most; a system to provide counseling and information to those who may be unfamiliar with or intimidated by educational institutions; a way to coordinate existing recurrent education programs to reduce duplication; and a mechanism to provide educational credentials to those who take advantage of recurrent educational opportunities.

Let us deal with subsidies first. A system of recurrent education vouchers, similar to the program being considered by the Massachusetts Legislature, is the keystone of such a policy.[6] The proposed Massachusetts Adult Recurrent Education Entitlement Voucher Program (AREEV) provides direct payments to mature adults who can then make their own choices about the services they will buy from existing recurrent education

---

[6]G. J. Nolfi and V. I. Nelson, *Strengthening the Alternative Postsecondary Education System: Continuing and Part-Time Study in Massachusetts* (Cambridge, Mass.: University Consultants, 1973), 4–7.

providers. This approach preserves the consumer orientation of the present system and does not supplant existing spending as a direct subsidy to the institutions might do. By focusing on the low-income client, the voucher program addresses a manageable problem of great social importance.

In addition, the proposed Massachusetts voucher program would be simply administered, and would eliminate deficiencies inherent in other subsidy proposals.[7] For example, the needs test is eliminated through the advance publication of eligibility criteria and the use of an audit procedure (similar to audits for income tax) with criminal penalties for cheating. In addition, the program is limited to the provision of instructional services. The voucher is designed on a per-course basis with a maximum limit of $50 per credit hour. This provision facilitates part-time study, the mode preferred by most adults. It is based on the premise that other services, such as information and referral, should be provided through agencies supported by public funds. Finally, the system uses a simple rationing scheme that solves two problems characteristic of student financial aid programs. First, there is no arbitrary cut-off, but rather a graduated voucher size that is based on income, previous education, and actual per-course tuition charges. As a result the middle class is not excluded from some aid under the program. Second, the design effectively offers most aid to those adults with the greatest need, while also providing some aid to adults with less need.

Eligibility based on both income and previous educational attainment is a major departure from financial aid patterns in traditional higher education. However, the nation has made a commitment to the provision of twelve years or the equivalent of free schooling to every citizen. An education-contingent voucher will permit those adults who did not take advantage of that commitment as youth to receive a relatively larger compensatory subsidy as adults.

While states have had the major responsibility for financing postsecondary education, recurrent education requires

---

[7]G. J. Nolfi, *State-Based Adult Recurrent Education Entitlement Voucher Program: Financing Open Learning and Continuing Education Through a Selective Entitlement* (Cambridge, Mass.: University Consultants, May 1975).

a mixed federal-state policy. This can be partially achieved through enactment of the National Adult Recurrent Education Entitlement (NAREEV) Program, which has been proposed before Congress.[8]

Next, let us consider counseling. The simple provision of subsidies to purchase recurrent education services will not meet the needs of the disadvantaged clientele. Many within this clientele are unaware of available services and are intimidated by educational institutions because of previous negative experiences. States should create and fund a network of community-based counseling centers located in poor and working-class neighborhoods. This action would provide an advocate to help those adults who believe the educational system is not for them or who do not understand its bewildering complexities. (A pilot statewide network of such centers has operated in Massachusetts since 1973.)

Although subsidies to institutions or particular programs generally are not required in recurrent education, the need for better information and referral is clear. Highly educated adults always seem to find what they are looking for, but disadvantaged and second-chance clienteles need help in designing a program for themselves, finding aid, and choosing among schools. An entitlement voucher program will not effectively encourage greater participation on the part of these groups unless supplemental information and referral services are provided.

Coordination, the third element of an effective recurrent education program, would be effected by a series of service area recurrent education councils. Creation of such councils would foster greater cooperation among all providers of recurrent education services within a geographic area such as a city, a region, or a metropolitan area. Such councils could coordinate and plan programs and foster a far more efficient use of all education resources within an area.

Finally, a set of competency-based credentials at all levels should be created and awarded independently of the existing

[8]G. J. Nolfi, *Proposal for a National Recurrent Education Entitlement Program: Financing Open Learning and Continuing Education through Selective Entitlements,* testimony presented before the Subcommittee on Postsecondary Education, House Committee on Education and Labor, Washington, D.C., September 25, 1975.

institutional and school structure. This action would give thousands of adults the opportunity to obtain a credential based on what they know rather than on how or where they learned it. Not only would this procedure restore some equity and legitimacy to learning in diverse settings; it would also provide an important incentive for those who have and can earn credits to continue in traditional degree programs for adults.

14

Speculating on Enrollments

Donald M. Norris

As everyone knows by now, the robust enrollment growth of the middle to late sixties did not carry over into the seventies. But not only have events in the past five years differed from those of the sixties, they have also failed to suggest patterns for the future. The net result has been considerable enrollment fluctuation and a basic uncertainty about the future. Both of these factors have exerted substantial impacts on planning and budgeting in higher education.

The average annual rates of growth in total enrollment of 6 to 8 percent that prevailed through 1970 dropped to 4.3, 3.0, and 3.9 percent in 1971, 1972, and 1973 respectively. Moreover, some types of enrollments actually diminished. In 1971, for example, total degree credit enrollments in two- and four-year private institutions declined, and first-time-in-college enrollments in all types of institutions dropped. In 1972, full-time,

degree-credit enrollment in two- and four-year institutions declined. Weaker institutions were hit especially hard by these
conditions.

By 1972, enrollment projections began to reflect a new
conception of the coming reality for higher education. A comparison of enrollment projections from several different sources,
which was first prepared in 1973, shows the now-familiar "go-
stop-go" pattern, popularized by the Carnegie Commission, of
increasing enrollments until 1980, then a gentle decline, followed by an increase in enrollments after 1990.[1] This shape
reflected a predominance of demographic trends, modified by
reasonably optimistic assumptions concerning how higher education would react to new educational realities.

Since then, enrollment fluctuations have continued. Students are selecting fields of study more oriented toward careers,
resulting in major shifts in the relative size of disciplines in
many institutions. Fall term, total enrollment jumped by 5.5
percent in 1974 and in 1975 it grew by the sizeable rate of 8.9
percent. While the largest gains were made by community colleges (nearly 20 percent), universities and four-year colleges,
both public and private, also experienced gains. Most observers
attribute the size of the increase to unfavorable economic conditions, which encouraged more students to enter college for
the first time, return after a hiatus, or refrain from dropping
out or stopping out.

The impact of these enrollment gains has been heightened by the fact that they were largely unpredicted, and the
mood concerning enrollments is far from sanguine. Many states
have been hit with enrollment increases at a time when economic recession has caused acute revenue crises. Regional variations
in enrollment conditions often make it difficult to apply national enrollment studies to state environments. One example is
Texas, which experienced enrollment increases of over 16 percent in 1975 and has prospects for continued growth in the near
future; another is the state of New York, which projects an undergraduate enrollment decline that will arrive sooner and with
greater severity than national projections suggest.[2] Also, a sig-

[1]W. L. Mangelson, D. M. Norris, N. L. Poulton, and J. A. Seeley, "National Enrollment Projections Studies," Planning for Higher Education 3 (1974).

[2]T. E. Hollander, Planning for Changing Demographic Trends in Public
and Private Institutions, ERIC Report ED 109 961.

nificant body of literature has begun to warn that underemployment and the saturation of the economy with college graduates will cause a drop in college attendance or a continuing increase in underemployment of college graduates.[3]

The net result of these uncertainties has been the appearance of a wide variety of projections of future enrollments. The trend-demographic projections in the 1973 comparison mentioned earlier portrayed a basically uniform concept of higher education. It was based on historical attendance patterns and projections of the size of a traditional age cohort, with some modifications made to accommodate higher education's reaction to changing conditions. The more recent projections present a variety of competing viewpoints that challenge the traditional concept of the higher education system.

Three recent Carnegie Commission projections illustrate the trend-demographic approach applied in a national setting. The 1973 Carnegie Base Projection predicts enrollments on the basis of Series E population projections and the assumption of a slightly decreasing high school graduation and college attendance rate.[4] The Carnegie Update modifies the earlier projection on the basis of the assumed attendance of larger numbers of nontraditional students espoused by the Carnegie report, *Toward the Learning Society.*[5] Both of these projections predict rising enrollments through 1980, followed by a fairly gentle decline until 1990, after which enrollments increase rather sharply through the year 2000. The magnitude of the difference between the two projections represents the projected impact of the modification (more nontraditional students). The third and most recent projection by Carnegie appeared in the Carnegie Foundation's report, *More Than Survival.*[6] It is based on Series F (now called Series III by the Census Bureau) population estimates and assumptions that enrollment rates for many

[3]S. P. Dresch, "Educational Saturation: A Demographic-Economic Model," *AAUP Bulletin 61* (Autumn 1975): 239-247; J. O'Toole, "The Reserve Army of the Underemployed," *Change* 7 (May 1975): 26-33, 63; and R. Freeman and J. H. Hollomon, "The Declining Value of College Going," *Change* 7 (September 1975): 24-32, 62.

[4]Carnegie Commission, *Priorities for Action* (McGraw-Hill, 1973).

[5]Carnegie Commission on Higher Education, *Toward the Learning Society* (New York: McGraw-Hill, 1973).

[6]The Carnegie Foundation for the Advancement of Teaching, *More Than Survival* (San Francisco: Jossey-Bass, 1975).

types of students will increase. This projection foresees rising enrollments through 1985, a weak decline through 1995, and modest growth thereafter.

A 1974 projection by Hollander forecasts a high and low figure for full-time undergraduates in the state of New York. While essentially a trend-demographic study, Hollander's projection isolates the effect of demography on traditional undergraduate enrollments and alludes to the impact of regional variation. If Hollander's projections are realized, the institutions in New York State will undergo a 20 percent or greater decline in traditional undergraduate enrollments by 1990.[7]

Stephen Dresch has been one of the leaders in attempting to link college attendance to economic rewards. His model suggests that continued high levels of college attendance will create a condition of "economic saturation." As a result, the declines in enrollments that may occur after 1980 may be far more severe than those projected by Carnegie. Moreover, the posited declines may continue even after 1990, albeit at a diminished rate.[8]

Richard Freeman and Herbert Hollomon have also investigated the impact that the recent, declining economic value of college-going may have on enrollments, with somewhat different results from Dresch. They suggest that the poor employment success of recent graduates may cause enrollments to peak sooner than the early 1980s, the time foretold by demographic studies. On the other hand, they believe that the decline in enrollments in the 1980s may not be as severe as predicted because the relative economic returns of education may actually improve during that period.[9]

Another variation on the economic viewpoint is reflected in several recent projections by the Bureau of Labor Statistics[10] and the National Science Foundation.[11] These studies attempt to project the supply of Ph.D.s in various fields, given the de-

[7]Hollander.

[8]Dresch.

[9]Freeman and Hollomon.

[10]Bureau of Labor Statistics, *Ph.D. Manpower: Employment Demand and Supply, 1972–85* (Washington, D.C.: U.S. Government Printing Office, 1975).

[11]National Science Foundation, *Projections of Science and Engineering Doctorate Supply and Utilization, 1980 and 1985* (Washington, D.C.: U.S. Government Printing Office, 1975).

mand likely to exist. In both projections, supply is projected to exceed demand in all major fields. The studies do suggest, however, that students will modify their patterns of behavior to narrow the gap between supply and demand.

Not all of the recent projections are so gloomy. Howard Bowen suggests that higher education may remain a growth industry, especially if "lifelong learning" becomes a reality.[12] If this occurs, he thinks it is quite possible that enrollments could increase by as much as 200 percent by the year 2000. Leslie and Miller also hypothesize more optimistically that higher education moves with a sort of "transverse progression" relative to the gross national product.[13] Thus if enrollment increase roughly approximates a rate of growth of the gross national product of between 2 and 3 percent per year, enrollments might increase by between 67 and 116 percent by the year 2000.

A further note of uncertainty is added by demographic reports from California that hypothesize that the fertility rate may be on the verge of bottoming out or increasing, after years of decline. The reason given is that many couples who merely deferred marriage and childbearing are now starting their families.[14] While such a condition would not affect enrollments directly until around 1995, indirect effects, such as an increased demand for elementary and secondary schoolteachers, could influence postsecondary education much sooner.

This group of projections presents a variation of viewpoints such as has seldom confronted educators. Taken together, they suggest that demographic and economic conditions will come to influence enrollments in new and as yet unpredictable ways, that regional variations will continue to be significant, and that the potential for adult learning may ameliorate potential enrollment declines. Yet it remains difficult to find unambiguous evidence in today's data that demonstrates conclusively how the future will evolve. For example, although the data on adult learning are improving, it is still not clear how extensive

[12]H. R. Bowen, "Higher Education: A Growth Industry?" *Educational Record 55* (1974): 147–158.
[13]L. L. Leslie and H. F. Miller, *Higher Education and the Steady State,* ERIC Higher Education Research Report #4, 1974.
[14]J. Sklar and B. Berkov, "The American Birthrate: Evidence of a Coming Rise," *Science 189* (August 1975): 693–699.

adult learning is and which institutions benefit the most. Many of the traditional institutions that are counting the most on burgeoning numbers of adult learners may benefit the least. Suggestions that the declining economic returns of education are driving students away are countered by the reality of increased enrollments in 1975, largely because of student reactions to an unfavorable job market. The result is that the problems caused by recent fluctuations in enrollments are multiplied by the problems attributable to a high level of uncertainty regarding future educational trends and enrollments.

The recurring fluctuations in enrollments are likely to continue, especially as institutions begin to compete even more actively for students.[15] Most of these fluctuations have severe impacts on short-term planning and budgeting. Combined with the high level of uncertainty concerning future educational conditions, they also exert a major impact on longer-term planning activities.

The budgets of many institutions have been hard pressed to meet the demands imposed by enrollment fluctuations over the past two years. While some states have provisions for withdrawing funds if enrollments fall short of projections, few will supplement appropriations if enrollments exceed projections. Thus, the largely unforeseen enrollment jump last fall has forced many institutions to support far more students on a fixed appropriation from the state. Michigan State University, a widely quoted example, had to educate approximately 3,000 more students than its appropriation accommodated.[16]

Students are flooding colleges and universities rather than the job market at a time when state revenues are least able to support them. State revenue crises in the Southeast, the Midwest, and the Northeast have forced states to prune their operations. In the process of cutting back, many states have been forced to abandon budget formulas and are relying on across-the-board cuts or politically motivated reallocation.[17] These cutbacks are imposing great burdens on the hard-pressed insti-

[15]J. K. Folger, "On Enrollment Projections: Clearing Up the Crystal Ball," *Journal of Higher Education* 45 (1974): 405–414.
[16]J. Magarrell, "They're Putting Lids on Enrollments," *The Chronicle of Higher Education* 11 (1975): 1.
[17]J. Magarrell, "Politics, Not Formulas, Now Cutting Budgets," *The Chronicle of Higher Education* 11 (1975): 1, 5.

tutions. The situation is exacerbated by the fact that many public institutions have been streamlining their operations over the past five years and have far fewer reserves of institutional resources with which to absorb greater numbers of students at stable levels of appropriation.

A further difficulty involves institutional adjustment to changes in student preference for academic majors. While keeping a certain percentage of their resources for new program development and innovation, institutions must also deal with the problem of shifting resources to increasingly popular professional and career-oriented fields without destroying excellence in more traditional disciplines. Given tight resources and demands imposed by year-to-year fluctuation, few institutions can deal adequately with this problem.

The reactions to most of these budgetary problems constitute a form of short-term planning. The nature of the fluctuations besieging state and institutional budgeting makes it difficult to determine if these fluctuations are one-time occurrences or the beginning of new trends. While it is possible to determine the demographic, economic, and public policy factors that will influence the level of educational enrollments, it is difficult to unambiguously predict what their influence will be. Will current levels of enrollment growth continue when the economy improves? Will shifts in student preferences continue? Institutions are confounded in predicting enrollments and budgets for next year or the next biennium and are uncertain about long-term educational prospects. It is especially difficult to focus on long-term issues when the short-term future is laden with intractable problems concerning dollars and enrollments. Unfortunately, the condition is made worse by the fact that tomorrow's enrollments are largely dependent on the planning and decision making that occurs today.

The natural tendency at times such as these is to temporize—to deal with short-term problems as they arise, but to avoid making long-term commitments. To the extent that this strategy keeps options open, it is good. But if it means avoiding all difficult problems and choices because of uncertainty, it is dysfunctional. An example illustrates this point. The recent projections by the Bureau of Labor Statistics (BLS) and the National Science Foundation (NSF) both predict the supply of Ph.D.s in life science will outstrip demand by 1980. However, the NSF projects a modest surplus of 7.7 percent while the BLS predicts a whopping 46.9 percent surplus. Rather than accept this considerable variance as reflecting the level of uncertainty inherent in the projection, graduate educators commonly tend to ignore both projections and to form their own ad hoc notions of the future.[18]

Part of the difficulty is that many of our scenarios of the future, especially those that use sophisticated modeling techniques, give the illusion of certainty.[19] In reality, these models are based on assumptions about the future. Merely because the model produces numbers and "hard" outcomes does not mean it is certain.

Under present conditions and in view of the variety of projections about the future, I believe the following planning strategy makes sense for institutions. First, educators should monitor the key demographic, economic, and policy factors that are influencing enrollments. Many of the data sources necessary to do this are available institutionally or nationally. In some cases—such as ascertaining the changing economic motivation for attending college among different groups of students—national surveys and samples may be necessary to provide expertise and resources not available to many states and institutions.

Second, if in their planning activities institutions and states use the models and analytical studies such as those of the Carnegie Commission, Dresch, and Freeman and Holloman, they must not ascribe certainty to the projected outcomes of these studies. Nor should they ignore a variety of models because their outcomes differ. Planners must also recognize that any decision-making activity that ultimately will result is likely to be judgmental, diffuse, and somewhat simplistic.

Third, the most valuable strategy under conditions of great uncertainty is one that maintains institutional options. Avoiding painting oneself into the proverbial corner is a mark of success in planning in such circumstances. However, liquidity and noncommitment do not connote just "muddling through."

[18]G. Kolala, "Projecting the Ph.D. Labor Market: NSF and BLS Disagree," *Science 191* (1976): 363–365.

[19]K. E. Boulding, "Reflections on Planning: The Value of Uncertainty," *Technology Review 72* (October/November 1974): 8.

The institution that properly monitors and evaluates leading indicators will know when to choose a particular course of action. The institution that merely muddles through may not receive the signal to move until conditions become critical. There is every indication that the penalty for such temporizing will be heavy, indeed, in the 1980s—and perhaps before.

Finally, it is important to reinforce Kenneth Boulding's assertion that the world moves into the future as the result of decisions, not plans.[20] The mere identification of alternate futures and relative levels of uncertainty is insufficient by itself. Moreover, the decision to maintain an open-option stance carries an especially heavy burden to continually review conditions in order to determine when it is prudent to choose a particular option. We cannot allow a high degree of uncertainty and enrollment fluctuations, revenue crises, and resource redistribution to divert all of our energies to short-term problems. Nor can we allow state government to singlehandedly assume the leadership role in redistributing resources in states forced to exist on limited resources. We must recognize that the fluctuations I and others have described will continue and will be joined in the 1980s—perhaps even sooner—by a confluence of demographic and economic factors that may cause fundamental changes in the size and nature of enrollments in postsecondary education. Our strategies for the last half of this decade must hinder neither our ability to cope with short-term difficulties nor our ability to plan for the longer range.

[20]Boulding.

15

Higher Education and Social Mobility

Engin I. Holmstrom

Higher education today is faced with three major difficulties, each of which threatens to enlarge the already dangerous breach between the public and the private sectors. Most conspicuous is the financial crisis. By this time, the refrain is familiar: The expansionist era has ended; hard times are upon us. As enrollments level off, as federal support dwindles, as private and foundation sources dry up, and as inflation eats away at institutional dollars, many colleges and universities find their very existence endangered.[1] Although the states have tried to

---

[1]See H. R. Bowen and J. W. Minter, *Private Higher Education: First Annual Report on Financial and Educational Trends in the Private Sector of American Higher Education* (Washington, D.C.: Association of American Colleges, 1975). See also L. H. Lanier and C. J. Andersen, *A Study of the Financial Condition of Colleges and Universities: 1972–75,* American Council on Education Special Reports (Washington, D.C.: Office of Administrative Affairs and Educational Statistics, American Council on Education, October 1975).

compensate for the decline in federal funds, it is unlikely that, as enrollment growth slows down, they can continue to provide increasing support to the public sector and at the same time come to the aid of private postsecondary education. Thus, the competition between the two sectors—for students and for federal and state monies—will probably intensify, to the detriment of both sectors.

The second difficulty besetting higher education is diminished public confidence in the value of a college education. Throughout its history, this nation has had faith in education as the key to the improvement of society and the betterment of the individual. But now, disheartened by the apparent insolubility of such pervasive problems as unemployment, crime and urban blight and burdened by inflation, high costs of living, government expenditures and taxes, the public has grown less sympathetic to the cause of higher education.

Unfavorable articles and books in the popular media—arguing that the soaring costs of a college education and the declining market value of a college degree make it pointless for most young people to invest either the time or money in an education beyond high school—have struck a responsive chord among a public that, for too long, has been "sold" higher education solely on the grounds that it brings increased returns on the job market. This skeptical attitude toward higher education is by no means shared by all. Many young people accurately perceive that without a college education, the opportunity to find work that is both financially and psychologically rewarding is not very great.[2] Their faith in higher education is well founded. Recent data from the Bureau of Labor Statistics clearly show that even in a recession, a college education still pays off in lower unemployment and better jobs. In March 1975, 2.9 percent of college graduates were jobless, compared with 9.1 percent of high school graduates and 15.2 percent of drop-outs.[3]

Nonetheless, higher education has lost some of its priority in public appropriations, and undoubtedly the loss of priority

[2]D. Yankelovich, *The New Morality: A Profile of American Youth in the 70s* (New York: McGraw-Hill, 1974), p. 28.
[3]"College Grads Still Have Job-Hunting Edge, BLS Says," *Higher Education Daily* March 3, 1976, p. 2.

is related to a lack of public confidence.[4] We need greater public understanding, yet it has become increasingly more difficult
to develop a consensus about the role and value of higher education—which brings us to the third major difficulty, the crisis
of purpose.

Higher education in America today has become a highly
complex, multipurpose enterprise, serving an increasingly heterogeneous population. The complexity of the system, the diversity among institutions, and the polarization between the
public and private sectors impede effective consensus building.
As David Henry has pointed out, we need "to find common
ground among the institutions of higher education as the basis
for public interpretation of purpose, achievement, and potential."[5] I believe this common ground is students. We need to understand more clearly the interaction between students and
institutions. We need to abandon our simplistic view of the distinction between the public and private sectors—which is primarily a political and not a functional distinction—in favor of
a more realistic concept of the nature of institutional diversity.
We have to concentrate on how institutional diversity relates to
and affects students. And we have to stop talking about students
in the aggregate.

In recent years, the student population has changed mark-
edly. As greater numbers of minority-group members, older
people, the financially and academically disadvantaged, women,
and part-time students enter higher education, generalizations
about the total group of undergraduates become meaningless.
For example, the notion that the college degree has lost its value
may be justified in the case of an economically privileged young
person to whom a college education (and subsequently an assured high-status job) was a foregone conclusion. But for lower-
income and minority students, a college degree can still make
a difference in what level of job opportunities are available.
(One possible consequence of the competition among recent
graduates in the job market may be the surge of applications to
elite institutions, a trend that suggests an effort to increase the

[4]D. D. Henry, *Challenges Past, Challenges Present* (San Francisco: Jossey-
Bass, 1975).
[5]Henry, p. 155.

economic distance between an "ordinary" degree and one from a more prestigious institution.)

Because the economic value of a college degree waxes and wanes with prevailing labor market conditions, a more stable benefit of increased education is social status. Higher education nullifies or greatly reduces the handicaps traditionally connected with sex, race, and age.[6] It also provides the credentials needed for career success. In recent years, colleges have provided credentials for the higher professions and also for many subprofessional and even technical occupations formerly learned through apprenticeships or in vocational programs in high school.[7] Postsecondary education, as the enlarged scope of the term suggests, may be the only societal force that lends itself to political manipulations intended to improve the life chances of citizens.

The remainder of this chapter will examine the extent to which higher education still promotes the upward mobility of a large number of students, permitting them to improve their social and occupational status. The analysis is based on data from the American Council on Education's most recent longitudinal undergraduate files, consisting of subjects surveyed first at the time of their college entry as first-time, full-time freshmen in 1968, and followed up four years later in the fall of 1972. These students entered a representative national sample of 358 two-year and four-year colleges and universities. Their responses were weighted to represent the total population of about 1.3 million first-time, full-time freshman enrollments in 1968.[8]

The phrase *first-generation college students* refers to those students whose fathers never attended a college or university. The phrase *second-generation college students* refers to those students whose fathers had at least some college education. The

[6]J. S. Coleman, "The Concept of Equality of Educational Opportunity," *Harvard Educational Review 38* (1968): 7–22; O. D. Duncan, "Inequality and Opportunity," *Population Index 35* (1968): 361–66; and W. H. Sewell, "Inequality of Opportunity for Higher Education," *American Sociological Review 36* (1971): 793–809.
[7]See Sewell.
[8]See A. Astin, *Preventing Students from Dropping Out* (San Francisco: Jossey-Bass, 1975) for a detailed description of the sampling and weighting procedures.

term *upward social mobility* is defined as the attainment of the baccalaureate by a first-generation college student. The analyses controlled for sex, race, ability, and income, all of which are related to degree attainment.

Ability is measured by high school grade averages: higher-ability students are those with averages of $B+$ or better; lower-ability students are those with B or lower averages. Higher-income students are those reporting parental incomes of $10,000 and above for 1967; lower-income students are those with parental incomes less than $10,000. Median splits were used for both the ability and income measures. Two categories were used to define race: blacks and nonblacks, the latter including not only whites but such nonblack minorities as Spanish-speaking Americans and Asians.

The analysis makes use of the Carnegie classification of postsecondary institutions because it allows for greater differentiation among types of institutions than the U.S. Office of Education classification.[9] Because the emphasis is on baccalaureate completion within four years after college entry, those institutions and programs that do not conveniently fit into this pattern are excluded—for example, two-year colleges and schools of engineering and technology. Thus, the study is based on students entering only the following Carnegie-typed institutions: doctorate-granting universities (including research universities), comprehensive universities, and liberal arts colleges. These institutions constitute about half the population of higher education institutions and serve over two thirds of the student population.[10]

Although the public sector served larger absolute numbers (three out of five first-time, full-time freshmen in 1968 enrolled in public four-year colleges and universities), the distribution of the students within each sector was strikingly similar. About 47 percent were women, 8 percent were black, and 39 percent were of lower ability. The major differences occurred with respect to parents' income and father's education: 46 percent of the students in the public sector, as compared

[9]Carnegie Commission on Higher Education, *A Classification of Institutions of Higher Education* (New York: Carnegie Foundation, 1973).
[10]Carnegie Commission on Higher Education, pp. 6–7.

with 35 percent in the private sector, were lower-income students. Similarly, 57 percent of the students in the public sector, as compared with 43 percent in the private sector, were first-generation students. First-generation students constituted just over half (52 percent) of the entering freshman class in 1968. Fully 70 percent of first-generation students as compared with only 57 percent of second-generation students attended public colleges. Income and race were strongly related to generational status in that three out of four lower-income students and nearly four out of five blacks were first-generation students in contrast to about one third of the higher-income and one half of the nonblack students. Sex and ability, on the other hand, bore little relation to generational status.

The distribution of first-generation students among institutions of higher education was not random, but followed a similar pattern in both the public and private sectors. That is, selective liberal arts colleges, followed by doctorate-granting universities, were least likely to enroll first-generation students. The highest concentration of first-generation students occurred in the public comprehensive universities and colleges category[11] and in the private, less selective liberal arts colleges.

Students in the private sector were more likely to earn the baccalaureate in four years than were students in the public sector. This was true for both first- and second-generation students: 62 percent of first-generation students in the private sector, in contrast to 54 percent of those in the public sector, and 68 percent of second-generation students in the private sector, in contrast to 59 percent in the public sector. Thus, the findings here lend support to the view that the public sector provides access to large numbers of students whereas the private sector, though its clientele is smaller, provides a more personal, individual educational service, with the result that a larger proportion of its students persist in college. Although students in the private sector were more likely to earn degrees in four years than their counterparts in the public sector, the pattern of degree completion rates within each sector was strikingly

---

[11]In the Carnegie classification, this is the Comprehensive Universities and Colleges II category, which includes 85 state colleges, most of which were formerly teachers colleges.

similar. In other words, the baccalaureate performance of students improved as one moved from doctorate-granting universities to comprehensive universities and colleges, reached a peak in selective liberal arts colleges, then dropped in the category of less selective liberal arts colleges.

Generally, second-generation students were slightly more likely to receive the degree than were first-generation students (63 percent versus 56 percent), but the generational difference in degree performance varied somewhat by sex, race, income, and ability of the student and by the type of institution. Some institutions seemed to cater to second-generation students. On the other hand, some institutions seemed to minimize the effects of academic, financial, and generational differences among their students. For instance, first-generation students in selective private liberal arts colleges were just as likely as second-generation students to receive the degree in four years; moreover, their baccalaureate completion rates were higher than those of students attending other types of institutions—a difference that persisted across ability, income, sex, and race categories.

The fact that over half the students entering the nation's four-year colleges and universities in 1968 were first-generation college students, and that four years later, first-generation students received nearly half the baccalaureates awarded to their class, has tremendous social significance. In a short period, higher education institutions provided the means of upward social mobility to over a quarter million students—many of whom were, at the time of college entry, "disadvantaged" in status. In four years, these students improved their status and their prospects. In a crowded college labor market, they enhanced their competitive position for a better job and a stable income.

For higher education and for the public, one important message conveyed by these findings is that college is still the major vehicle of social mobility and personal fulfillment for millions of Americans. Recognizing that fact and using it as a springboard for improved services to all kinds of students may help restore financial support, confidence, and a sense of purpose to higher education.

16

Learning and Earning

Juanita M. Kreps

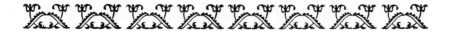

The seeming mismatch between what a college graduate has learned and what the labor market calls for has become a national concern. The poor fit plagues Ph.D.s as much as B.A.s and for those students who would themselves become educators, the future looks worse, not better.

Higher education has traditionally met different needs for different people. To students it has offered rites of passage and the first taste of freedom from family constraints; to parents, the promise of upward family mobility—a promise for which many families have made great sacrifices. Society's expectations have been even greater: as a nation, we have looked to higher education for a better tomorrow through greater social, scientific, and technological knowledge.

For a long time, few were skeptical of higher education's ability to deliver on these promises. No one doubted the wisdom of spending for education, and some even demonstrated that such investments bore higher rates of return than investments in physical capital. Costs of education were considered low,

155

relative to the price of ignorance. And so we allocated a growing portion of a growing national income to higher education.

Now the dream is shattered. There are voices in the land questioning the wisdom of putting dollars into higher education rather than into health or the environment or business. Inevitably, the crass question is raised: Are we getting enough back from our education dollars? Would we be better advised to give our children the appreciated value of their education allowance instead of the depreciated value of a degree? Perhaps the most extreme view comes from Caroline Bird, who argues that college is "the dumbest investment you can make" and cites as proof the well-known compound interest exercise: a Princeton student who invested the $34,181 cost of his degree at 7.5 percent interest compounded daily would have $1,129,200 at retirement, or about half a million dollars more than the average lifetime earnings of a college graduate.[1]

Another analysis that gives little reassurance to the economy-minded educator is provided by Paul Taubman and Terence Wales.[2] Their examination of the impact of education on earnings—specifically, on the earnings of a cohort of males who were born between 1916 and 1926, and who in 1943 had at least a high school diploma—reveals some startling facts. An undergraduate degree lifted annual earnings in current dollars by 31 percent, but for those with some graduate work (but no graduate degree) the increase over high school earnings was only 26 percent. A master's degree yielded a 32 percent increase but a Ph.D. only 27 percent. In law and medicine the differentials were three to four times those accruing to undergraduate and graduate degrees: 84 percent for the LL.B. and 106 percent for the M.D. Social rates of return to educational investment, deflated by the consumer price index, were not high: from high school to some college, 11 percent; to the B.A. degree, 8 percent; for some graduate work, 5 percent; to a master's degree, 6 percent; to a Ph.D., 2 percent; and to an LL.B., 9 percent.

For those who would justify higher education on the basis of its contribution to earnings, there is more bad news. Attempt-

---

[1]C. Bird, *The Case Against College* (New York: David McKay, 1975).
[2]P. Taubman and T. Wales, *Higher Education and Earnings* (New York: McGraw-Hill, 1974).

ing to isolate the effect of education, by itself, on earnings, Taubman and Wales separate (as best they can) the contributions of mental ability, family background, age, marital status, and health from those of quantity and quality of education. They find that poor health cost a man $7,000 in 1969 earnings; being single cost him $3,000. The variable for marital status, incidentally (usually interpreted as a proxy for motivation and need for income), is not simply significant; its coefficient is actually larger than the effect of the education or ability variables. In other words, for those who want to make money, being married is more important than being educated! As the father's education rose, so did the son's annual earnings. For example, a man whose father had a bachelor's degree was likely to earn $4,000 more than a man whose father had never gone to high school.

Of the abilities included—in mathematics, coordination, verbal skills, and spatial perception—only mathematical ability (primarily numerical fluency and only secondarily problem-solving competence) had a significant influence on earnings. Furthermore, "the pretest variation in quantity and quality of schooling had little effect on test scores or earnings . . . Thus, the ability coefficients should be closer to measures of the effect on earnings of inherited mathematical ability than anything else." The earnings of the men who ranked in the highest fifth in ability were 15 percent higher than the average high school graduate earnings in 1969; those in the next highest ability group earned 2.9 percent more. Ability had little effect on earnings at the beginning of work life, however, and later appeared to be most effective for those with graduate education and very high levels of ability.

Two other findings are of particular interest. First, the quality of education (judged on the basis of the Gourman Academic Rating) has a significant effect on earnings. Depending on their college's quality, the earnings of males with three-year graduate degrees varied between 53 and 98 percent above the earnings of high school graduates. Second, the screening effect of education on earnings is quite high, accounting for perhaps half the increase in income. This finding bolsters the authors' conclusion that there has been an overinvestment in education; before-tax returns on most physical capital run 13 to 15 percent and thus greatly exceed the usual social rate of return to education. Since the rate of return declines with additional years of study (except for the study of law and medicine), the overinvestment is particularly marked in the case of the M.A. and Ph.D. degrees.

A word on methodology. In their detailed analysis of the determinants of earnings, Taubman and Wales draw on a data set that is unique: a longitudinal sample of 5,000 men who, having volunteered for the Army Air Corps, were surveyed in 1943, again in 1955, and a third time in 1969. Having at least a high school diploma and with test scores at the college sophomore level, this cohort of males was more intelligent (and less averse to risk) than average. The authors are careful to warn that some of the results, drawn from a sample of a special population, may not be generally applicable.

But the more important caveats have to do with what is being measured. Can research identify the nonpecuniary returns to education? Is it even measuring the financial returns accurately? As we continue to probe the relationship between education and other factors such as health, demographic characteristics, and the taste for leisure, and between preschool environment and school performance, what will we find to be the most significant returns for an investment in education? We may discover that the financial rewards are small indeed to the average student. Broader questions for research are also raised: What types of abilities influence subsequent performance, and how are these abilities to be measured? Can we determine what cognitive or affective skills are improved by education, and how?

Taubman and Wales acknowledge that a further look into the black box called education could reassure educators, but their tentative conclusions are these: personal characteristics and mental abilities contribute as much to earnings as education; the real rate of return on a college degree is only about 8 percent; approximately half of that return is caused by the screening effect of education.

A more recent study paints an equally dismal picture of the decline in earnings of college graduates.[3] Richard Freeman

[3]See the review article, R. Freeman and J. H. Holloman "The Declining Value of College Going," *Change* 7 (September, 1975): 24–62.

and J. Herbert Hollomon report that between 1968 and 1973
the starting salaries of male graduates fell 23 percent for social
science and humanities majors and 21 percent for math graduates, measured in constant dollars. Similarly, male college
graduates earned 53 percent more than high school graduates
in 1969, but only 40 percent more in 1973. The rate of return
on college investment fell from between 11 and 12 percent in
1969 to between 7 and 8 percent in 1974.

In explaining this marked decline, Freeman and Holloman cite several factors, most importantly a leveling off of professional and managerial jobs as a percentage of all jobs, and
a sharp rise in the number of college graduates seeking these
higher-level positions. In the 1960s, there was an annual growth
in the college manpower-intensive sectors of 4.4 percent; in the
early 1970s the growth was 2.8 percent. Education, and research
and development, two of the big consumers of educated talent,
fell significantly as shares of the GNP. On the manpower supply side, however, growth in numbers was the highest in history:
an 8 percent annual increase in number of new B.A.s on the
market between 1968 and 1973, as compared with a growth of
1.75 percent annually in the sixties. As a result of the labor market imbalance, unemployment rates were sometimes higher for
college than for high school graduates. These trends may account in part for the fact that the proportion of eighteen- to
nineteen-year-old males enrolled in college declined from 44.0
to 33.4 percent in the five years from 1969 to 1974.

Although Freeman and Hollomon expect the problem to
persist through most of this decade, they see some market improvement in the early eighties, with a stabilizing of demand
and supply by the late eighties. They warn that the return of
full employment will not reestablish the historical differentials
between high school and college graduates, however, and that
intergenerational mobility will not necessarily be upward in the
future.

These new studies do not improve the image of higher
education in the eyes of prospective students or their parents,
but neither do they necessarily lower the status of a college education. The claim that higher education guarantees financial
or professional success to graduates, or even Ph.D.s has never
been reliable. It is not even clear that the hope for career suc-

cess has been the motive for going to college. Students have always been wise enough to realize that most of what will happen to them out there in the world will be influenced by factors that are unpredictable. They know that going to college might or might not pay. But for many it is still the only game in town.

Recently a Duke undergraduate reminded me, with some edge in his voice, that I had apparently forgotten the message contained in the university's bulletin, a message he said had persuaded him to enroll at Duke. The words are William Johnson Cory's: "You go to a great school not so much for knowledge as for arts and habits; for the habit of attention, for the art of expression, for the art of assuming at a moment's notice a new intellectual position, for the art of entering quickly into another person's thoughts, for the habit of submitting to censure and refutation, for the art of indicating assent or dissent in graduated terms, for the habit of regarding minute points of accuracy, for the art of working out what is possible in a given time, for taste, for discrimination, for mental courage and mental soberness."

17

Academic Hypocrisy: A Media View

Noel Epstein

There is much gloom these days about the problems facing higher education. Fears abound that a good number of colleges and universities will be forced to merge or close over the next decade. Many people are worrying about dwindling job openings for college graduates, increased political influence in campus affairs, the drying up of opportunities for young professors, lowered academic standards, the financial squeeze on angry middle-class families, the decline in funds for basic research, and much else.

But one of the most critical questions—one that is far more fundamental to my mind than precisely how many campuses may or may not disappear—has not received serious attention. It is simply the question of academic hypocrisy, of a community of men and women devoted to intellectual honesty who are increasingly seen—often with good cause—as not practicing

161

what they preach. Nothing, I think, can have sadder consequences for the academic world or for an already distrustful and troubled nation than a flourishing of hypocrisy among truth-tellers, a turning to expediency in hard times among those who speak of principles.

Yet that, I believe, is what has begun to happen. How can educators complain that government is undermining the merit system when grade inflation is rampant and honors lists are close to meaningless at many schools? How can educators sneer at commercial advertising methods when their own brochures often bear little resemblance to what happens in class and when apprehensive schools resort to slogans, gimmicks, and marketing men to lure more students? How can academics urge federal regulation on everyone else in society and then howl when faced with regulation themselves? How can scholars who cloak ideological positions on significant national issues as scientific research speak of a dispassionate quest for truth "wherever it may lead"?

Obviously these and other contradictions between word and deed do not apply to everyone in higher education today. There are certainly distinctions to be made among institutions and among individuals. But the inconsistencies are sufficiently widespread to make them a serious problem for the entire academic world. In small ways and large, they erode the very authority and purpose of higher education.

Academic promises are no longer sacrosanct. Students who feel they have been bilked by false advertising are taking their grievances to the courts. One student, for example, recently sued the University of Bridgeport in Connecticut for $400 over a teaching-methods course that she claims was "worthless" and "ridiculous," teaching her little more than how to work an overhead projector. Another student dragged George Washington University to court over a landscaping class that she termed "pure junk"; she settled privately with the school, getting back part of the tuition she had paid before dropping out. The complaints of these two students are unusual only in having been among the first to reach the courts. The basis of the complaints is widely recognized even in academic circles. It was stated succinctly by K. Patricia Cross: "The curriculum statement printed in the catalogue frequently bears only the faintest resemblance to what is taught by faculty."[1]

The pressure for truth in advertising is going to create increasing problems for campuses, especially for campuses in financial trouble and campuses striving to attract more and more students beyond traditional college age to ease their nightmares about empty seats. In both the Connecticut and Washington cases, it should be noted, the complaining students were married women returning to class after an absence of some years. Like them, many older students with jobs and families must sacrifice a great deal to go back to school. They will not accept so easily any of the "breeze courses" that undergraduates sometimes seek out to escape too much work. Older students will demand specifically what the catalogue promises, and some schools will either have to rewrite the catalogue or require faculty to fulfill the promise.

Pressures are growing and will in fact continue to grow in the entire area of consumer protection in higher education. It is a sad day when colleges and universities require reminders of the need for truth in advertising or in anything else, but that day is already on us. Congress is well aware of this problem. Representative James O'Hara, the Michigan Democrat who chairs the House subcommittee handling higher education legislation, believes that "Truth-in-advertising is as appropriate in the catalogue of a distinguished university of ancient lineage as it is in the television advertising of a trade school."[2] His committee has been considering a measure to extend such regulation to all Office of Education student aid programs. This indication of congressional concern should serve as fair notice to all colleges and universities to stop using gimmicks, slogans, and other questionable pronouncements that mislead students.

I am troubled, for example, by the "career education" slogan. I am not even sure what "career education" means, but its growing popularity, particularly at financially strained cam-

[1] K. P. Cross, "Learner-Centered Curricula," in Dyckman W. Vermilye, ed., *Learner-Centered Reform* (San Francisco: Jossey-Bass, 1975) p. 54.
[2] J. O'Hara, *Congressional Record*, February 20, 1975, p. H969. Remark made in introducing his Student Financial Aid Act of 1975.

puses, suggests that it improves the chances of graduates to find good jobs. The notion that "career education" will lead to more careers for the college-educated is, of course, sheer nonsense. The same number of graduates will be underemployed or unemployed no matter how extensively "career education" spreads across the country.

Besides, is the higher education community seriously suggesting now that it has not long been involved in career education, if that means equipping people with marketable skills? It would be nice to think that all those students have been attending college chiefly to acquire knowledge for knowledge's sake, but this obviously is not so. Most have been after the material or psychic income of higher-status positions, and campuses have no control over how many of these positions will be out there waiting for new candidates.

Probably the most enduring consequences of "career education" will be to make further inroads into liberal arts studies and to improve the ways in which some schools already provide career skills along with broader education. It is not clear to me, though, exactly how many employers are really seeking graduates who are less well rounded than their predecessors but who have some additional skills. Many employers may prefer to teach skills on the job. The *Washington Post* editorial department, for example, looks with suspicion on applicants who have majored in journalism as undergraduates. It prefers those with wider backgrounds, more flexibility, an ability to deal with complex questions involving judgment and discretion and imagination. This may not be typical, but I imagine that a good number of corporate, government, and university employers are not searching for more narrowly educated staffs.

There are doubtless areas where more skills may help students compete better for jobs. But for many the proliferation of "career-oriented" studies in communications, business, premedical, or whatever subject will constitute a hoax. It will neither expand the number of opportunities nor necessarily make the graduates more attractive job applicants. And it certainly will not advance the emerging generation's sense of justice or history or other perspectives that were so sorely lacking among those highly skilled individuals involved in the Watergate affair and in other recent blemishes on our national record.

When our own words come back to haunt us, some think it wiser to change what is preached rather than what is practiced. This change has already occurred in some academic quarters with respect to federal regulation. Ten years ago there was no educators' chorus complaining about red tape or expensive data-gathering required by Washington. On the contrary, the dominant theme in those days was that federal regulation was greatly needed. This, however, meant federal regulation of others, principally of business and union officials, who also had to shoulder the paperwork and other heavy costs of compliance. Now one hears not only educators' complaints about bureaucracy and expense but also assertions that an effort such as affirmative action in higher education threatens the merit principle, or that campuses know better than government how to correct their past sins—which, of course, is what the corporations and unions said.

Higher education's social sympathies seem to have changed overnight. In 1969–1970, when the Labor Department required contractors on federally financed construction projects to seek 20 percent minority workers, there was little campus outcry over this action. I remember noting this silence not long afterward to a prominent New York intellectual and academic who had by then become a severe critic of affirmative action, especially as applied to campuses. His reply, as best I can recall, was, "We changed our minds," accompanied by a shrug. We all have the right, and sometimes the wisdom and courage, to change our minds, but his sudden new faith struck me as one of the more convenient conversions I had run across.

My purpose is not to examine the many arguments being advanced about affirmative action, but only to make a few observations about academic statements on the issue. One concerns the frequent contention by some that "goals and timetables" are really "quotas." They are not. The simple reason is that no campus has ever been threatened or penalized by the government for not meeting a specific goal or timetable. The dispute today is over how to draw up such plans, not about how to fulfill them. In fact, the only quotas that are a reality in higher education are those created by colleges and universities themselves. Some undergraduate and professional schools have claimed the right to set quotas for minority admission, an issue currently before the courts again in several states. It is difficult to comprehend how campus officials can declare that a department's standards of merit should be strictly adhered to in faculty hiring but that preference by group membership should be given in student admissions. They cannot have it both ways.

Finally, I would like to raise what is to me the most serious problem of all: scholars who mix rhetoric with research on profound national issues. However good their intentions may be, they mislead the nation and damage their own authority when they confuse political apples with scholarly oranges. Many scholars themselves are deeply concerned about this. Richard C. Atkinson, deputy director of the National Science Foundation and former head of Stanford University's psychology department, remarked in a recent interview: "Some social scientists want to run the goddamn country, and that's an unhealthy attitude."[3] He said elsewhere that he has heard fellow psychologists "too often speaking on issues of education, child rearing and mental health using what they claim to be research evidence as a disguise for advocating a particular policy."[4]

Atkinson would like to see researchers who are more interested in politics and power than in science run for public office. He believes that "anyone coming out of the college system should be able to question social scientists, to say, 'Show me your data and forget your interpretations.' " Above all, he would like to see more systematic challenges to research affecting public policy.[5]

Others have also been pondering "corrective devices," ways to curb any unwarranted influence that social or physical science reports and pronouncements may have on our lives. These include proposals for simultaneous studies done for opposing interest groups; restudies of existing research, a complicated technique currently being funded by the Russell Sage Foundation; and triallike hearings or review panels to hold researchers to the same high standards of proof on public issues

[3]N. Epstein, "The Scholar as Confuser," *The Washington Post*, February 15, 1976, p. kl.
[4]R. C. Atkinson, "Psychology—Reflections on Its Past and Concerns About the Future," Temple University, Philadelphia, October 30, 1975.
[5]Epstein, p. kl.

as on strictly scholarly ones. Some scholars, such as the conservative Columbia University sociologist Robert Nisbet, have even suggested that science and government should be entirely severed from each other. Science's aim, he has remarked, "is *not* to advise governments, save mankind, make public policy or build empires," but the "search for truth, the discovery of data, principles and laws to enlarge our understanding of man's purpose."[6]

There is no reason why scholars should not examine immediate issues, should not tell us, as far as possible, the likely consequences of alternative national policies or how existing programs are working. This information can only help to enlighten the debate on all sides. The trouble begins when the country starts expecting much more, and when scholars start believing they should oblige. In most cases, science cannot answer the questions of morality, justice, or politics at the bottom of our national dilemmas, no matter how much a shaken nation may yearn for scientific certainties. Nor can scientists instantly agree on what should be learned about a public issue before decisions are made and lives affected. To be reliable, the scientific process long has required that others challenge one's findings and chip away at theories over time until some accord can be reached. Advocacy is neither a short-cut to truth nor a substitute for scientific consensus.

A classic case of the confusion that results from mixing advocacy with science is the controversy over sociologist James S. Coleman's study of school desegregation and white flight.[7] Coleman has been attacking many courts, pointing to his widely disputed research finding that desegregation leads to a "sizable" exodus of whites to the suburbs or to private schools.

But the heart of his quarrel with federal judges is not about white flight. He is not opposed to court-ordered busing as one way of undoing unconstitutional segregation. He does not think his study is even relevant for courts where busing or any other device is needed to undo illegal segregation.

---

[6]R. Nisbet, "Knowledge Dethroned," *The New York Times Sunday Magazine,* September 28, 1975, p. 89.

[7]J. S. Coleman, S. D. Kelly, and J. A. Moore, "Trends in School Segregation, 1968–73," paper prepared by the Urban Institute, Washington, D.C., August 1975.

What, then, has the national storm been all about? It has been about a personal Coleman position that does not carry any scholarly authority.

As Coleman remarks: "I am sure there is confusion between what I say that is based on my research and what I say that is not based on my research results—which stems in part from the research and in part from a particular philosophy of education."[8]

The personal position Coleman is espousing actually goes well beyond "a particular philosophy of education" to a fundamental question of justice, and it has relatively little to do with sociology. He is chiefly quarreling with courts in some cases over their definition of "illegal segregation" and in other cases over whether the remedies the courts order exceed the offenses found. Only where judges agree that they are *unjustly* ordering busing does Coleman think they should weigh the degree of *unnecessary* white flight he sees being provoked.

A rough analogy in a criminal case would be if a social scientist believed two parents were unjustly convicted of murder and then executed—and then told everyone that this procedure increases the number of orphans in the country. Naturally. But the chief complaint would be about justice, not orphans, just as the chief argument in Coleman's case is about justice, not white flight.

Similar questions can be raised in the dispute over nuclear power plants and safety, in which scientists have signed petitions on both sides, or in the argument over depletion of the ozone layer, in which scientists do not have enough information as yet to agree on very much.

The scholarly community runs great risks if it loses sight of the fact that its primary search is still for truth, however imperfect that quest. Advocacy is appropriate only after all ideological and scientific sides of an issue are presented in their works. At present, even conflicting findings of a strictly scientific nature on public issues are given scant attention by many researchers. In the Coleman case, for example, his final draft of last August relegates to a footnote a contradictory work by Reynolds Farley of the University of Michigan, who used the

[8]Epstein, p. kl.

same government data but different methods of analysis. While Coleman found that desegregation leads to a "sizable" exodus of whites from public schools, Farley found no significant relationship between the two.[9]

Coleman acknowledges this problem. "In the policy area," he states, "I think it's true that this report and other reports in the social sciences are relatively blind to other research. I think this should be corrected, that it should be part of the change in the way research which is policy-related is presented."[10]

All this is to say nothing of the recent Senate disclosure that several hundred academics are engaged in clandestine activities for the Central Intelligence Agency. It is a woeful comment on the times that academics should need reminding that they cannot pass off propaganda as research, that they must disclose the source of their funding, that they run grave risks if they transmit to the CIA the confidences of colleagues or students. There is certainly nothing wrong with aboveboard work and contacts with the CIA; there is something horribly wrong with the covert CIA work.

The inconsistencies that combine to make up academic hypocrisy are not just another problem faced by higher education today. They are the source of many of the difficulties associated with decreased public confidence in higher education. That confidence is not likely to be restored until colleges and universities set a high example of integrity. We badly need our scholars and teachers. We need their knowledge, their guidance, their thirst for dispassionate inquiry, their commitment to the search for truth. If we cannot find these in the academic world, where can we turn?

[9]R. Farley, "School Integration and White Flight," paper presented at the Symposium on School Desegregation and White Flight, Brookings Institution, Washington, D.C., August 15, 1975.
[10]Epstein, p. kl.

The CUNY Experience

Timothy S. Healy

The City University of New York (CUNY) has ten senior colleges and ,eight community colleges. Along with two graduate colleges, these eighteen enroll some 250,000 students of which about 180,000 are undergraduates. Open admissions began in 1970 and means, simply, that CUNY will find a place for any graduate of a New York City high school, public or private. The entry ticket is a high school diploma. Students in the top half of their high school class or with an 80 percent average have been admitted into senior colleges; students below these levels into community colleges. During 1975–1976, counting both terms and including transfers, CUNY took in 70,000 first-admit students. In 1969, before open admissions, the total was closer to 35,000.

The first change the program brought to CUNY, naturally, was in size. One college president, peering out over his packed campus, quipped, "We're all right till it rains!" In 1970, fully 30 percent more of New York City's high school graduates applied for college than had applied in 1969. Whatever our admissions policy was before 1970, a lot of people seemed to have had the impression that they were not welcome.

Open admissions brought not only greater numbers but also greater diversity than ever before. The university's minority percentages rose from roughly 10 to 30 percent. The most surprising single fact about the new students, however, was that seven out of ten were from the white ethnic mass of the city's high schools. Equally surprising, at least to the critics of the program, was the fact that the brighter graduates, the students with averages in the high 80's and 90's were not turned off or away. These students continued to enroll as they had in the past.

Apart from introducing a large stratum of remedial courses, open admissions really had very little effect on the college curriculum. In most details that curriculum has remained pretty much what it was in 1960 or even in 1950. One significant change was the gradual shift in the late sixties from required to optional courses, from table d'hote to cafeteria. That change was based on a double premise: first, that freedom is good for the soul, and second, that the students in the process of greening America know better than the faculty what they need. Open admissions had little to do with this particular failure of adult nerve, and was, in fact, more harmed than helped by it.

The entrance of black experience into the curriculum also owes little to open admissions. This work was well begun before 1969, and the 75 percent increase in black students may, at most, have accelerated the process. This is not meant to imply that the short and simple annals of the underprivileged now loom large as a curricular component. But at least one battle appears substantially won. At no future date will American historians, critics, sociologists, political scientists, or economists ignore what black Americans have accomplished, suffered, and contributed.

The profound change that the introduction of over 30,000 Hispanic students into a university might have wrought has simply not occurred. The curricular history of the world as most young Americans have it presented to them consists of the doings and misdoings of two great empires: the Roman and the British. These are followed by the American empire, which, of course, denies that it is one. The fact that between the first and second of these enterprises there occurred a third, as large and as influential as either, would come as a surprise to many of our students. The entire world of Spanish exploration, colonization, work, and understanding is a closed one in American higher education. This omission endears us to our neighbors south of the border, and contributes in no small way to the tact and success with which we conduct our affairs in our neighbor continent. The slow chipping away of the curriculum by Spanish-speaking students has largely been a matter of getting their language accepted. It is, after all, the speech that Charles V claimed was the finest developed by man for his three essential occupations: praying, cursing, and making love. But the social, political, spiritual, and artistic wealth that lies behind that language has yet to have much impact on American academic practice.

A third area in which open admissions has had less impact than expected is the racial composition of the university's faculty. In all probability, the work of the affirmative action program has contributed more to faculty diversity than open admissions has. It is true that open admissions did provoke two years of frantic hiring that added a number of minority group members to the faculty. But these people were hired mainly for remedial courses, which have generated tenure far more slowly than other courses of study and, in addition, have been more vulnerable to financial crunches. The sad fact is, there are still very few credentialed black and Puerto Rican candidates for faculty positions. Graduate schools are in the process of remedying this dearth, but as so frequently happens with America's address to racial problems, the ground rules change just as opportunity beckons.

Although changes in the university itself were modest, much has been learned from open admissions. First, we learned how to "remediate" in simpler terms, how to help young adults cope with reading, writing, and arithmetic. That does not sound like much, but the process took at least five years. It took, and is still taking, a scholarly analysis of street speech so we can learn where impedence patterns lie; and while we have come a long way with English, we are just beginning with Spanish. There is in all this a great deal of pious posturing, even among those who should know better. Letters to the editor come pouring in protesting the horror of high school graduates with eighth-grade reading skills. Nobody bothers to point out that a ninth-grade level is average for college freshmen across the nation. New York City's high schools, while they are clearly the most publicized, are not necessarily the worst.

A second place where the university learned lessons from open admissions was the whole scale of points between "the revolving door" and "the great wall of Princeton." Any urban university must, as the financiers who run our lives say rather grossly, stay liquid. When open admissions began, CUNY was afraid of making the whole thing an empty gesture, by luring students in only to flunk them out. The university has been told patronizingly by several institutions that they had had open admissions for a long time. What they neglected to mention was that their freshman instructors were told to fail 40 to 50 percent of every freshman class. Legislators were kept happy by the admission of the sons and daughters of constituents, and the faculty was reassured that the ill-prepared were safely "cooled out" in the freshman year. This situation was, of course, an eventuality that CUNY wished at all costs to avoid, so much so that, instead of the revolving door, the door was nailed shut in several colleges. Once a student was in, it was almost impossible for him to get out. The university began by saying that no student should be dismissed for academic deficiency in the first two semesters. This rule meant that three semesters would have to go by, and for students with heavy remedial (and thus non-credit) loads, three semesters could take a long time. It became apparent that we were approaching the idea of tenured students. We have learned the lesson, and are correcting the balance on the side of severity.

Something else we have learned is not to wince when someone mentions standards. There is, of course, a great irony in the current debate about standards. The minute one says the word, one enters the world of codes. Just to complicate the problem, the word works differently in several different codes. For instance: it is acceptable for Yale University to talk about "grade inflation" and for other major universities to acknowledge, somewhat shamefacedly, that 65 to 70 percent of their students are making the dean's list. But it would be a public disgrace for CUNY to acknowledge either. What for Yale is a *faux pas* is for CUNY a felony.

On the other hand, there is no evidence that CUNY's bachelor's degree has declined in value or in demand. There is evidence that some students achieve it with extraordinarily low averages. They are almost as low as the "gentleman's *C*" that dominated American higher education in the days when one believed that gentlemen peopled Wall Street. As a matter of fact, the open admissions students have probably been the most totally self-selective in the history of American higher education. Seven out of ten of them are in the community colleges, and not in the senior colleges. The vast majority of them are there because they want to be. Knowing what they knew on coming out of high school, they quite rationally decided, "Let's approach this thing carefully." So when it came to dipping a toe in the academic pond, they picked a quiet place in which to do so. Even within the community colleges, the academically nervous (and the underprepared) tend to group in technical and career programs rather than in liberal arts programs. Five out of seven poorly prepared students who go to a community college will track themselves into career programs, where they feel less reading, writing, and mathematics will be required.

The combination of open admissions and free tuition provided a laboratory for studying something else of interest. If urban students face neither an academic nor a financial penalty, they will take their education in considerably smaller doses than students normally do. The average time for completing a bachelor's degree at the City University of New York is not four years but six and a half. Interestingly, that is the average for all students, those who come in with a 90 average from the Bronx High School of Science as well as those who score 60 at Benjamin Franklin. It is not only that most students work. More to the point are the rhythms of life in a great city, which make most students feel more comfortable dropping in, dropping out, and dropping in again. The interstices are filled with lots of activity, in which one hopes that growing up is included.

Not all we have learned from open admissions has been encouraging. In fact, one finding confirms our worst fears. Of the 70,000 students who pour into CUNY each year, about

15,000 need deep remediation. Once it has been given to them, 5,000 of them will succeed, 10,000 will not. For open admissions students, success in college means that they arrive in the upper half of whatever program they are following with no further need of extraordinary help. They can float on their own, finally and fully. Whether or not they are happy while so floating is a question that no college can answer, and that probably none should ask. What defeats us is how to identify and help the 10,000 who will not succeed.

Another puzzle that remains unsolved after seven years of open admissions is what the university's relation should be with the city's embattled high school system. The areas where open admissions might have brought about change within the high schools are three: the numbers going on to college, the numbers staying in high school to graduation, and the skills level of those who do graduate.

Open admissions did work a major change in the number of students continuing on to college. The total jumped from 50 percent to 70 percent of the high school graduating class. Thus the program provided an outlet in which the students were interested, that their faculty encouraged them to take, and that they took in larger numbers than ever before (and in larger numbers than any other place in the nation).

When we come, however, to the other two areas the results are considerably less startling. As far as anyone can tell, open admissions has had little or no impact on the tremendous exodus that occurs between the middle point of the eleventh grade and the end of the twelfth. It has been estimated that fully 50 percent of the black and Puerto Rican high school students who have survived into the eleventh grade will drop out between that point and the end of the twelfth. Open admissions, even by limiting admissions to those who have diplomas, has had little impact upon that loss.

In the final area where open admissions could have had an impact on the high schools, in skills, there seems to have been almost none. Whether or not the instrumental skill of high school graduates—their ability to read, write, and do basic calculations—has declined since the open admissions program began, no one can say. There seems to be little evidence that it has declined, despite the claim of some school officials that decline is the inevitable result of lowering the barriers to college admission. What is painfully clear in every college in the system and from every teacher who has had to deal with students who come to us is that their basic instrumental capacity has not at all increased.

What can be done to curb the drop-out rate and to improve the skills of the high school students? It seems to me there are three principal steps that must be taken. First, the regents of the state must be encouraged to do what they have been talking about for years, that is, set a minimum standard level of competence in both language and arithmetic. This standard would take a great deal of pressure off the high schools, and would mean that the high school diploma indicated a basic ability to read, write, and calculate. Second, with the cooperation of the high schools, the university should move its testing program down to at least the tenth grade. This move could start the admission cycle (including advanced placement) working early. It could provide an early warning system for students and their parents. It could enable the high school to work out remedial programs for those who need them most, and to do so well before the end of the twelfth grade. It could also enable the university, in its admissions, to honor progress and momentum as well as a rather dubiously measured attainment. Finally, the university must continue to make available to the high schools all that it has learned about remediation, as well as to make available the people who have made the learning possible. In addition, it must try harder than it has in the past to adapt its teacher training to the needs of the school system. Brooklyn College is already a pacesetter in this and the rest of the system should follow. The following, however, may indeed be hard. It may mean, for example, that teacher trainees will have to learn Spanish to teach in a system in which one third of the pupils speak Spanish. Unless the university is willing to take such steps, its position is quite literally untenable.

These, then, are some of the things the university has learned from 75,000 students who, as conventional wisdom would have said, should never have been admitted. Twenty-five thousand of them will make it through to a degree. For these students the results are not yet in, but are quite immeasurable anyway. There is a terrible fascination about the 50,000 who will not make it through. If open admissions is stopped, there are going to be some 5,000 to 7,000 students a year, who, in their turn, will not make it through either. In one way or another our society is going to pay for their lost opportunity. Some of them will, of course, scramble out of the trap on their own; many more will not. So in welfare, in prisons, and in hospitals we will make the payments we refuse to make in college.

Each year CUNY has spent about $30,000,000 on its open admissions students. Over five years, that comes to $150,000,000. If that amount pulled 25,000 young citizens out of the poverty cycle, each pull cost $8,000. There are a lot of other ways to spend $8,000. Two of them leap to mind: eight thousand dollars is about one year of welfare or six months of prison. Future historians are not going to be hard put to see how inexpensive the city's chief assets, its children, really were.

And if the money is not available, if open admissions is finally called off, we academics who watched it succeed will mutter, as academics have been muttering for some centuries, "This thing worked; Eppur, si muove."

19

Ethnic Studies in Cultural Perspective

Richard Gambino

I n 1974 I conducted a survey of ethnic studies in American higher education for the Rockefeller Foundation.[1] About 135 colleges and universities offered ethnic studies at that time. (Lower school systems in thirty-three states also offered them.) The type, organization, and quality of the programs and courses varied greatly. I found courses about single ethnic groups, courses about several ethnic groups, and courses about ethnicity as a category of human life. The scholarly standards of the offerings range from excellent to incompetent and propagandistic.

These courses are often outside the usual "catalogue" offerings, although some social sciences and humanities departments are attempting to integrate ethnic studies into their

[1]Free copies of this report, *Guide to Ethnic Studies Programs,* are available from the Rockefeller Foundation, 1133 Avenue of the Americas, New York, New York 10036.

conventional courses. In some cases, the courses are supervised by the usual department or college committees. This arrangement favors maintenance of high scholarly standards. But sometimes the committees' inertia and hidebound biases inhibit innovation. On the other hand, independence from the usual academic structure provides freedom, which has been abused conspicuously in some cases.

A principal reason for the confused, poorly organized status of ethnic studies is that they are highly controversial among administrators, faculties, students and the public. Ethnicity itself is highly controversial in America.

Controversies about ethnic studies in American schools have been marked by emotions and perceptions that are transient, personal, and biased. These need to be balanced by rationales (pro and con), premises, principles, ideals, and standards in order to provide a firm foundation for ethnic studies.

For many years now, cultural anthropologists have employed concepts that will be used here to scrutinize relevant American social and historical realities. In 1926, Bronislaw Malinowski first introduced the concept of "charter myths" held by peoples. These myths are the mostly unquestioned systems of root beliefs, styles, and values that underlie behavior. They define a people and distinguish one group from another. In order to appreciate fully the issues surrounding ethnic studies, we need to examine the character of the charter myths making up our "mainstream" culture. We also need to analyze dominant myths of American education that pervade schools from the nursery through graduate levels.

It is a commonplace that traditional "mainstream" American culture is derived mostly from the charter myths of the white Anglo-Saxon Protestant (WASP) group, and especially from the upper-class segment of the WASP group. These WASP charter myths traditionally formed and sustained things "typically American," from cachets of dress, grooming, and mannerisms to complicated opinions, values, institutions, and behavior.

Other groups, and the individuals comprising them, have confronted these mainstream WASP charter myths with varying results. Non-WASP *individuals* have gone along one of two paths, either seduced or coerced by intense melting-pot pressures. All individuals have been affected. It is impossible even for the staunchest individuals in the most isolated environments in America to remain uninfluenced by elements in the larger society. Some non-WASP individuals have adopted merely the superficial behavior styles, only the visible surfaces of the WASP charter myths, while retaining and developing other, even discordant, charter myths in their lives. These individuals have *adjusted* to the WASP charter myths, but have not undergone assimilation. They suffer internal conflict, either visibly or "in the closet."

Other individuals have gone the more complete way of *assimilation*. They have truly appropriated the WASP charter myths as their own cultural and psychological cores. It is a process that of necessity takes several generations. Yet, even assimilation is limited. Obviously, nonwhites can never completely assimilate—a fact that much of America has finally accepted. But the same is true of Slavic-, Jewish-, and Italian-Americans, among others. Ethnic history is as undeniable as racial background. As Horace M. Kallen put it in an article published back in February 1915, "men may change their clothes, their politics, their wives, their religions, their philosophies, to a greater or lesser extent; but they cannot change their grandfathers."[2]

Groups (as distinct from individuals) have confronted WASP charter myths with several types of results. Of all the larger ethnic groups in the United States, perhaps only Irish-Americans, Jews, Asians, and blacks have achieved some degree of respect for their charter myths from the WASP elite. In a hard-won struggle, Irish-Americans, Jews and Asians have gained limited (very limited) "mutual validation" of charter myths with WASPs. Each of the groups concedes that the charter myths of the other group are valid for that group, while fully retaining and developing its own charter myths. The mutual validation between WASPs on one side, and Irish-Americans, Jews, and Asians on the other is concomitant with the latter groups "making it" in higher education. This can be seen in the results of a 1974 study by Andrew Greeley.[3] This study showed the following order of ethnic groups at the top in per-

[2]H. M. Kallen, "Democracy Versus the Melting Pot," *The Nation*, February 18, 1915, pp. 190–194.
[3]A. Greeley, *Ethnicity in the United States* (New York: Wiley, 1974).

centages of college graduates: Eastern European Jewish 27.5
percent, other Jewish 26 percent, German Jewish 23.3 percent,
Asians 20 percent, Irish Catholics 14 percent, and British Protestants 13.6 percent. At the other end of the scale are blacks
with 4 percent, Spanish-speaking background 4.1 percent, Slavic
5.1 percent, Polish 5.1 percent, and Italian 6.1 percent.

An important corollary to the partial mutual validation
between Irish-Americans, Jews, and Asians on one hand, and
WASPs on the other, is that the former are the only non-WASP
groups permitted to be themselves (to a limited degree), to retain and develop their own charter myths, and also be fully
American in the decisive American mythic environment.

Blacks are the only other group moving toward mutual
validation with WASPs. (Other "nonwhites"—American Indi-
ans and Latin-Americans—have gained status as favored minorities in the wake of the black movement but do not appear
to be moving toward mutual validation.) Irish-, Jewish-, and
Asian-Americans have forced some recognition of their culture
as legitimately American by long, hard-won, competitive educational and economic success within the mainstream social
systems. Blacks, on the other hand, with competition more effectively closed to them for so long, have forced WASP validation of black charter myths through massive social protest,
agitation, and disruption, which began in the 1950s, climaxed
in the 1960s, and continues at high pitch in the 1970s.

The other groups, "out in the cold," have had to grant a
greater or lesser degree of "unilateral validation" to WASP
charter myths. In this one-way process, the validated WASP culture does not reciprocate by validating the charter myths of the
outgroup. Unilateral validation results from large numbers of
people from the subordinate groups assimilating, not just adapt-
ing to, the charter myths of the dominant group. The only options allowed members of a group on the subordinate end of
unilateral validation are either to assimilate fully or to remain
something less than fully legitimate Americans. The inevitable
result in unilateral validation is extinction of the subordinate
ethnic group.

The confrontation of non-WASP groups with WASP charter myths has also led to a third type of relationship, that of
mutual *in*validation. This is a mutual denial by each group of

the other's charter myths. Most ethnic groups, especially those of Southern and Eastern European and Latin American background, are in this relationship. Despite the fact that all individuals in these groups have adapted to WASP charter myths, only a minority of them have assimilated. These individuals are offered two options: assimilate, or remain second-class, "backward" Americans. The first option offered to groups in this relationship is to give in and unilaterally validate WASP culture, and thereby to suffer extinction as groups. The second option is to maintain and evolve their own identities outside the mainstream and thereby remain subordinate in the powerful American social myth hierarchy.

It is no mere coincidence that the American social hierarchy exactly fits Protestant British biases. The relative status of ethnic groups in the United States is virtually identical to the feelings of Protestants in Britain toward other peoples in the world. The traditional order of these feelings, from positive to negative, is: Northern European Protestants, Central European Protestants, Western European Catholics, Southern and Eastern Europeans, Latin-Americans, Asians, and Africans. The fact that this hierarchy is still strong in the United States is evidence that WASP charter myths still form our "mainstream."

It should be noted that when other powerful social movements enter into the American social process, they usually adjust to and perpetuate the ethnic hierarchy and its patterns of validation. The women's movement of the 1970s is a good example. Those women who are rising through affirmative action favoritism appear to be WASP, Irish, Asian, Jewish, or black—mutual validation functioning. They include a handful of other women—unilateral validation and assimilation operating. Unassimilated women from other groups are not favored—mutual denial operating.

Of course, social and economic class are powerful determinants in American life. But here, too, class operates in and through the framework of the ethnic charter myth hierarchy. American social scientists, with their nineteenth century model of world dynamics as "rational" (in the sense that Marx used the concept), overlook this fact. Yet class in America does not function exclusively through such rational movement. Other, irrational determinants remain critical and are not destroyed by class as Marx predicted. Many social scientists have belatedly recognized that race is among them. They have yet to concede that ethnicity is also included.

Generally, an American is permitted to rise economically to a degree directly related to the status of his ethnic group. And he is permitted to rise socially according to the degree to which he is assimilated. As a rule, merely adjusted individuals are not given access to the highest social strata. (The question used to evaluate wealthy or prominent people from invalidated groups when they apply to the elite clubs is illustrative: "Is the applicant typical of his ethnic group in his occupation, life-style, dress, and behavior?")

When we turn to the world of American education, we find that it merely reflects American society as just described. Despite the view many academicians have of themselves as avant garde, liberal social reformers, they conform to the prevailing ethnic hierarchy and patterns of mythic validation. As is true of the boards and officers of major foundations and the higher executive ranks of large corporations, patterns among college administrators and ranking faculties perfectly match the hierarchy. In education, highest power and position is held predominately by WASPs, with a very limited share given to Irish-Americans, Jews, and Asians, and with increasing numbers of blacks quickly being moved in. The few individuals from other groups in higher positions are, with rare exceptions, highly assimilated. The merely adjusted remain in the lowest or peripheral ranks—or altogether outside.

American colleges have always engaged in ethnic studies, albeit unwittingly. Today, the form and content of the education they offer is largely molded and sustained by WASP charter myths, with the very restricted influence of Irish, Jewish, Asian, and black charter myths. The WASP charter myths determine what is to be researched, taught, studied, and discussed on campuses. They also dictate what "objective" criteria, values, opinions, and standards are to be worthy of serious consideration.

Thus, English departments in required courses teach British literature as the birthright of all Americans along with American—that is, WASP—writings, and a mere sprinkling of Irish-American, Jewish, and black works. Literatures in translation, from Italy, Poland, and Latin America, are rejected as "foreign." The content of humanities courses is heavily made up of WASP concerns with some small representation of the concerns of the other validated groups. The products and concerns of all other groups are pejoratively labeled "ethnic" and ignored. Thus, for at least a generation now, Jewish studies have been regarded as a serious academic pursuit—but on only a few campuses. And only in recent years have black studies been tolerated. The claims of other groups for ethnic studies, their requests for inclusion of their cultures, histories, and charter myths, are met with impassioned recitations of melting-pot litanies, ridicule, or cavalier dismissal.

The existence of Catholic colleges confirms rather than alters this analysis. These colleges stand on the short end of a unilateral validation relationship with the ethnic charter myth patterns held in secular colleges. And within the Church schools themselves the prevailing charter myths are of Irish-American and, to a lesser degree, German-American cultures. Charter myths of other Catholic groups are denied validation and individuals from other groups are pressured to adapt to or, preferably, assimilate Irish-American charter myths.

Still another myth prevailing in American education is that of "universal culture." This myth is partly a vestige of eighteenth- and nineteenth-century enlightenment. It is also partly a continuation of the turn-of-the-century mentality that mobilized the American educational world to achieve a melting pot, that is, to anglicize and protestantize the millions of new immigrants. The goal in the universalist myth is to distill a "higher culture," purged of all origins and pure of all distinctions of nationality, race, ethnicity, and class. Exclusive attention is accorded the elements of this pure culture. Of course, the pursuit of pure culture is a bald absurdity in the light of insights from contemporary anthropology, sociology, and psychology. And the notion that the elements of universal culture "already discovered" are other than the products of WASP charter myths is a monument to the failure on the part of the universalists to examine their own deepest assumptions.

American education is, in the name of a will o' the wisp universalism, an instrument that endorses fully the validity of WASP charter myths, gives very limited endorsement of Irish,

Jewish, Asian, and black charter myths, and invalidates all others. It is, thus, a major party to the suppression of all other ethnic groups and the effort to extinguish them as such, and to the pressure to force all individuals from invalidated groups to deny their identities by adjusting to or assimilating the "valid" charter myths.

These functions of American schools are indefensible, unless one is prepared to argue for the a priori cultural superiority of the favored ethnic group over all others. In addition, the refusal of competent faculty members to participate in ethnic studies because of the influence of the system of myth validation has left a large part of the field in the hands of incompetent enthusiasts, propagandists for various ethnic chauvinisms, and mere opportunists. These alone are good enough reasons to develop ethnic studies—studies more representative of our society, of a more consistently high quality, and with more and better faculty participation. But there are also even more compelling reasons.

A frequent accusation against ethnic studies is that they are merely "fronts" for ethnic chauvinisms, and some courses and programs are. These exist to spread the message that one ethnic group is superior to others, that membership in that group is proof of highest worth. Their effect is to parochialize people and alienate groups from each other. They provoke the traditional American fear of social fragmentation. Historically, that fear has resulted in great melting-pot campaigns, which press WASP charter myths on everyone while systematically suppressing all others.

Yet ethnic awareness need not result in parochialism and chauvinism. An educated knowledge about one's ethnicity can be creative. It equips a person with critical elements of identity. Moreover, a scholarly study of other ethnic groups gives insights into them and into ethnicity as a basic aspect of human life. Such study provides a basis for positive appreciation of other groups' "peculiarities," and sounder, less biased judgments about their cultural contributions to America. To establish this awareness, the present ghettos wherein members of an ethnic group teach about it or study it must be opened. The only criteria for researching and teaching ethnic studies should be professional competence, and the only requirements for study should be interest and the possession of any disciplined grounding that may be necessary.

Excellent ethnic studies are socially as well as individually creative. They lead to an atmosphere in which the potential contributions of all ethnic groups can compete fairly for attention and appraisal by American society as a whole. These contributions can then be appropriated by America, or rejected, on their merits. Fair appraisal is presently impossible because all charter myths except the validated ones are neglected and castigated as divisive and parochial, and as threats to American ideals. (The mechanisms of suppression are uninhibited in their prejudice. Thus, educated, liberal-minded Americans, who are too moral to tolerate anti-Semitic or antiblack stereotypes any longer in movies, television, and print, enjoy with clear conscience such malignings of the "dumb Polack"; the criminal or vulgar Italian; the "greasy," childish Greek; the racist, reactionary white ethnic—all standard fare in the media.)

The cultural pluralism that would result from good ethnic studies would enrich our common culture, as well as remove hypocrisy from the melting-pot ideal. Such a pluralism would not build walls between people. It would establish for the first time equitable relations between them. The goal, as John Higham has put it, is a society in which each ethnic group can preserve its cultural core, but whose cultural borders will remain open and receptive to other groups. In other words, the first ideal is of mutual validation and interchange between all groups.

The high social stakes involved in educators' attitudes toward ethnic studies were aptly put in an article about cross-cultural studies by Everett Kleinjans:

> *No one culture explores the total range of ways to organize life and express ideas and emotions. The teaching of other cultures as new ways to view the world is an excellent means to help people grow into more complete human beings, more understanding and empathetic, more able to get along with others. . . . On the other hand, what if we could develop a world (or a nation) in which there is a basic uniformity of values, customs, beliefs, and behavior? At that stage mankind would no longer be able to explore the total spectrum of possibilities for orga-*

nizing human life on this planet. To that extent, we might very well become psychologically and culturally poorer, rather than richer.[4]

Ethnic studies can lead to creative ethnicity in individuals and to a more just and rich American culture. Whether they will do so depends on the response by administrators, faculty, and students who have so far shunned them. To paraphrase Churchill, seldom has a call for educational leadership been incumbent on so many, and understood by so few.

[4]E. Kleinjans, "A Question of Ethics," *Exchange 10* (1975): 25.

20

The Case for Experiential Education

Morris Keeton

How would you like to fly in an airplane piloted by someone who had learned to fly entirely by reading books, hearing lectures, and discussing and writing about flying? How would you like to try to teach children to read entirely by reading to them and talking to them about reading rather than leading them through the experience of reading, reading, and more reading? How would you like to have a secretary whose training had been attained only from reading about secretarial services, seeing videotapes of other secretaries at work, and hearing lectures on the subject?

The answers to these questions are obvious. First, the use of experience in learning is essential to the achievement of most skills, and a high level of proficiency is possible only when experiential learning has been incorporated as central to the strategy of instruction. Second, an experience relevant for one learning objective will not be relevant for some others. Therefore, an experience-based strategy of instruction should consider using those experiences that exemplify the skills to be mastered or the understandings to be gained as outcomes of the learning effort. If the intended outcome is reading skill, the experiences that are critical are reading experiences. If the intended outcome is high competence in piloting aircraft, the experiences must be actual or effectively simulated piloting. If the intended outcome is quick apprehension and retention of the key ideas in a lecture, the experience must be one of hearing and repeating to other people the key ideas of some lectures.

Now, a second set of questions: How would you like to be treated for heart trouble by a doctor whose license to practice rested on test scores rather than evidence of having examined or successfully treated cardiac patients, or even observed other doctors examine or treat cardiac patients? How would you like to be defended by an attorney whose license to practice and subsequent qualifications derived from examining processes and other criteria none of which included evidence of the attorney's having served as advocate or participated in the advocacy of persons accused of crimes? How, as a citizen, would you like to be served by public officials and representatives whose credentials in critical thinking were based on an examination process rather than on a demonstration of their performance as critical thinkers on novel issues in an actual arena of public controversy? (Why do I ask that question as if it were a contrary-to-fact hypothesis?) The point of these questions may be less obvious than that of the first set, but it is no less compelling. A credential that does not rest on an experiential test of performance or on reliable evidence of competent performance is not worth the paper it is written on. Credentials are not trustworthy if they are not linked to experience-based assessment.

It does not follow that every learning task can be mastered by simply practicing it over and over. One cannot learn to fly by being strapped into a Boeing 747 without prior preparation and having been told how to fly the thing. Nor can one learn mathematics by being given a problem in differential calculus and told to practice on it. There are subtleties to the strategies of instruction and there are trade-offs between bearable risks

and costs on the one hand and the benefits of genuine experience on the other hand. Some learning tasks, moreover, are
prerequisite to others, and some skills can be useful as tools for
learning many other things.

We have, in higher education, hardly begun to exploit
the possibilities of more imaginative and more effective mixes
of experiential and theoretical instruction and of experience-
based assessment of learning outcomes. As a teacher of critical
thinking skills, I have found no strategy that approaches in effectiveness the combination of two things: an enormous number
of student attempts to think through increasingly complex problems that differ in content and context; and the use of a variety
of resources—conceptual, informational, and instructional—at
junctures in the experiential procedures where a readiness to
reflect on the subject matter of learning has been heightened
or sharpened by the experiences. Strategies designed to these
specifications are almost sure to elicit deeper understanding,
greater motivation and energy to learn, and a more precise
grasp of data and concepts than strategies that rely only on doing or only on being told. As a certifier, moreover, I can be much
more confident about predicting the nature and quality of performance by the licensee if I have observed the person in a variety of performances under varied circumstances within the class
of tasks in question.

Let me cite one further experiential example, based on
my association with credentialing at Antioch College. The most
sophisticated of Antioch's ventures in the assessment of the
learning of complex and difficult tasks is probably its current
venture at the School of Law. The lawyering capabilities certi-
fied include interviewing skills, analytical skills, and negotiating skills. Such skills rest on capabilities that should flow from,
or emerge in the course of, a liberal education—for example,
the ability to make well-grounded political and ethical judgments and to adhere to them reasonably well in one's conduct;
the ability to write a well-reasoned argument or brief for a position; the ability to communicate clearly and persuasively through
the spoken word; and the ability to grasp the critical elements of
a culture or social environment, to understand the functioning
of normal and of deviant individuals within such an environment, and to apply this understanding to the rights of an ag-

grieved or an offending party. My belief is that none of these capabilities can be developed by a person to the level of that person's potential without substantial use of experiential learning strategies.

Most colleges have been content with half a cake. They have wanted students to understand cultures, but not deeply enough to become astute judges of causation or insightful inventors of ways to ameliorate social problems or cope with individual life crises. Or they have aimed at creating effective speakers with respect to grammar and rhetorical style, but not persuasive communicators in a complex social situation. The Antioch Law School experience, though still very limited and incomplete, convinces me that it is possible to achieve a depth and sophistication of learning far beyond what present standards require or contemplate.

The premises of experiential education are strikingly simple. First, quality *education* must include experience in the tasks to be learned; second, first-rate *credentials* must be based on experience; and third, we have hardly begun to apply vision, imagination, and sophistication to the design of instructional and credentialing strategies that combine experience and theory. What is less simple is bringing about the institutional changes necessary to translate these premises into practice.

21

Equality and Success

M. Elizabeth Tidball

Men and research. They go together. They are what we all think of when we respond to questions about the success of individuals and the greatness of institutions. They have come to symbolize higher education in the United States; for many, they are sacred symbols.

Academics have been running hard and fast for the past twenty years, but few have questioned the direction. Most have assumed that the highest good came from research endeavors, not realizing, or failing to face the fact that the ladder of success was being scaled mostly by men. We have begun to pause a bit in our race, however. We see that it is time to take stock. Almost overnight we have wakened to a world in which the goals and values of higher education are being challenged. This world seems suddenly to have acquired large numbers of people called "women" and "minorities" who want not only jobs but also status. The familiar fertile soil that once grew money trees now lies fallow from accumulated pollutants. We slow down to catch our breath. Where are we? What are we doing? Did we run too far in the wrong direction? Where do we go from here?

Perhaps we can find our way by remembering that there was a time when virtually all persons who aspired to careers in higher education pictured themselves as both teachers and thinkers. The mix could vary at any given time, and, depending on the material supports required for thinking, each function might be carried on sequentially rather than simultaneously. For example, the biologist's summer trek to Woods Hole supplemented the abstract thinking that went on during the school term; and a Christmas vacation spent in the reading room of the British Museum gave impetus and critical references to the paper brewing in the historian's mind the preceding autumn. Lacking these supports, the college library and the interchanges among faculty colleagues were always available to expand one's mind and enrich one's teaching.

Conversely, the concentration and involvement in teaching served to stimulate the thinking of professors as well as of students. Expressing ideas out loud to others, even if they are not one's own, or explaining to someone else how to do a chemistry experiment reveal new insights to the teacher even as he or she transmits facts to the student. And coming to grips with the questions and observations of students naive in the teacher's own world can raise questions for future thinking. This view of the scholar-teacher not only prevailed as recently as the 1950s; but its idealization and societal affirmation also led many of us to choose our life work as teachers and thinkers.

It would be impossible to enumerate the multiplicity of events, discoveries, and exigencies that overlapped and coalesced to change the academic world so radically some twenty to twenty-five years ago. A vignette from my own life suggests the unfolding drama. The alarm went off at three a.m. and my husband and I, silent but very much alert, moved into the routine laid out the evening before: start the water boiling for the hot chocolate; pull on the old wool ski pants and warm jackets; pick up the binoculars and the Thermos; wake up Bob and Holly; set out in the bleak, clear night for the empty lot at 57th and Drexel; and wait and watch. Soon, across the still-dark sky, eerily and precisely on schedule, moving inexorably—too rapidly for an airplane, too slowly for a shooting star or comet—across that Chicago sky and easily visible without the binoculars, Sputnik I entered our lives. We did not know then the extent to which it would influence our future as teachers and thinkers, or the roles of institutions, or the whole fabric of society. The star of science and technology had been revealed, and we responded collectively as did the Wise Men of old: "We have seen his star in the east and are come to worship him."

So science and technology grew and grew and grew. Federal funding was generous beyond comprehension, and apparently inexhaustible. The number of men earning science doctorates jumped from 14,000 in the 40s to 75,000 in the 60s, an increase of more than 500 percent. Women, too, entered the sciences in greater numbers: 4,700 earned science doctorates in the 60s compared with 1,150 in the 40s, for an increase of 400 percent.[1] A great discrepancy is apparent, however, between the numbers of women and men receiving science doctorates. Whether one considers the past fifteen years, or the fifty-five years for which uniform records have been kept by the Doctorate Record File, men earning science doctorates comprise about 43 percent of all doctorates, and women some 3 percent. Ergo, research scientists are men. So are research scholars in all fields, but it is the sciences that have been the major beneficiaries of federal largesse during the years of heavy government involvement in higher education. The money and the action were to be found in the natural sciences. And the status and the power. And the men. Higher education took on the distinctive flavor of men and research.

Noting this paradigm of success, academics in the arts and humanities began to model themselves after the scientists, that large group of men researchers who got the money and called the shots, who were courted by the best institutions to join their faculties, and who brought new prestige to many a lesser institution. Institutional quality, once determined on the basis of selective admissions, began to be defined in terms of doctoral production, to wit: American Association of University Professors (AAUP) groupings of Category I, Category IIA, Category IIB, and so on. Paralleling these assignments of research status are faculty salaries, highest for each rank, regardless of geography, in Category I. Although many educators insist they

---

[1] *Doctorate Records File,* Board on Human-Resource Data and Analysis, Commission on Human Resources, National Research Council, National Academy of Sciences, Washington, D.C.

are not playing the game of categories and dollars, most, in fact, are. Approximately 86 percent of all men and 77 percent of all women who teach in four-year institutions are to be found in research-oriented schools (where, however, the ratio of men to women faculty is about 4 to 1). These simple facts of demography and institutional definitions have affected our thinking about our roles, our values, and our self-worth.

Other factors, too, influence our perceptions and our behavior. In an era of objective measurements and standards, research accomplishment lends itself far more readily to evaluation than does teaching expertise. At first we tried to evaluate ourselves by number of publications. Soon the humanists picked this method up and equated one book to two or three journal articles. Then we realized that sheer numbers were inconclusive, so we added the citation index, the number and order of authors listed, and the stature of the journal or publisher to our list of criteria for research accomplishment. "Publish or perish" became an all-important game with a multitude of subtle and intricate rules—but almost everyone played.

Students also contributed to the teaching faculty's pursuit of research. The rapid infusion of students into higher education, starting with the influx of servicemen following World War II, increased the number and diversity of our constituency, and hence too the complexity of the teaching enterprise. When the mid-sixties erupted in student protest over social and political issues, faculty found a haven in their disciplines rather than in institutional commitment. Discipline orientation, and the research required to meet the approbation of peers within the discipline but outside the institution, provided isolation from the turmoil, as well as the opportunity for regaining the self-esteem that had been diminished by student alienation.

I shall never forget attending, as a spectator, the opening convocation at a small liberal arts college in the fall of 1968. The ceremony was held outside and so the audience sat in the chill darkness, each of us wrapped in a kind of friendly separateness, awaiting the official words that would tell us an opportunity for a new beginning was at hand. No one around me knew me. For a moment I fancied myself a new faculty member with no prejudged conclusions about this community I was becoming a part of. What were the students like? And my colleagues? What sort of impetus would be generated at this first gathering to start us off together in our teaching and thinking and learning? The formalities began: the academic procession of faculty, seniors, the officers of the administration. The chaplain stepped forward to say the invocation. It is beginning, I thought, and my heart actually quickened. And the chaplain said, "Lord, we know our government is in the wrong, our president is in the wrong. . . ." I was stunned. I was very much alone. I felt a sense of unbelonging overwhelm me. In that brief instant I realized I had come to the wrong place, had made a grave error in judgment. But I found the answer to my disaffection almost as quickly as I had become disaffected. My discipline, my research. If this man represented the college's posture of scholarliness and inquiry, if to this man had been entrusted the first impressions of new faculty and students to the community, then I wanted no part of it. My sense of profound alienation and aloneness was relieved as I walked back to the local hostelry for a cup of coffee and realized, first, that I was only passing through, and, second, that my laboratory and my research can provide me with a splendid isolation any time the immediate world of students or colleagues or deans comes too close for comfort. I am not certain I like what I learned that autumn night in 1968, about myself and my profession. Research involvement speaks to a multitude of profound questions.

Our glorification of science and research has worked its way into our value system not only at the institutional level but at the personal level as well. This is not idle speculation. During the past year I have been analyzing the 1973 American Council on Education Survey of Teaching Faculty. The data, obtained according to institutional type and by sex, indicate a strong, positive correlation between men's self-ratings of success and affiliation with research-oriented institutions, meaning that the men affiliated with teaching-oriented institutions rate themselves lowest in self-esteem.[2] This finding is all the more revealing when one realizes that men who teach in four-year coeducational colleges overwhelmingly believe that teaching, not published

[2]For a more complete treatment of methodology and data, see M. E. Tidball, "Of Men and Research: The Dominant Themes in Higher Education Include Neither Teaching nor Women," *Journal of Higher Education 47* (July-August, 1976).

research, serves as the basis for promotion; yet their self-esteem rides on the research image of their institution rather than on its teaching-oriented reward system. The male-research-prestige triumvirate appears to influence all men in the comparisons they make between themselves and their peers.

Women faculty generally do not gain their sense of success from affiliation with research-oriented institutions. This is, of course, realistic on their part. Even for women who are active researchers there is a considerably looser linkage between their accomplishments and the reward system. We have known for some time, for example, that women are paid less than men at every rank, that they tend to cluster in the lower ranks, that they are the mentors for fewer research students on a per capita basis, and that they receive fewer grant dollars and fewer national achievement awards. So it is not too surprising that they would not base their assessment of professional success on the research image of their institutions.

What, then, generates self-esteem in women? This question is not as simple to answer as it is for men. First of all, women in general rate themselves considerably less successful than do men. Secondly, self-esteem in academic women depends on whether they are comparing themselves with men or with other women. When they compare themselves with men, women are more likely to identify their affiliation with teaching and with issues of concern to academic women as the bases for their sense of success. Women who teach in women's colleges compare themselves most favorably with men, while those who teach in private coeducational colleges record the lowest self-ratings. But when women compare themselves with other women, the criteria change. Women who rate themselves the highest in such comparisons are those most closely associated with men who feel more successful than other men: these are the women who teach in the traditionally all-male institutions and private universities. Their basis for self-esteem is therefore derivative rather than original.

What is apparent is that men, the dominant group, set the tone for what is important in the academic world; and what is important to them in terms of feeling successful is their affiliation with research-oriented institutions. By contrast, women's definition of success is not confined to professional, academic

success. It may include the idea of success as a human being in
a wider context. Yet standing outside the system as women do,
they downgrade themselves. The tight bond of maleness, research, and prestige excludes them by definition not only from
institutional affirmation but also from their own sense of worth
as academics.

One consequence of these patterns of self-esteem is that
students find themselves being taught by faculty who devalue
teaching or devalue themselves. As one might expect, however,
the men students fare better than the women. Further data
from the American Council on Education (ACE) survey indicate that both women and men faculty are more supportive of
students of their own sex than they are to the opposite sex. And
since the number of men faculty far outweighs the number of
women faculty, the climate for men students is more cordial.
In addition, the concern of men faculty for issues relating to
women in the academic world—issues of discrimination, anti-
nepotism rules and the like—is considerably less than that of
women faculty. So along with their greater affirmation of men
students generally, men faculty are not in tune with issues that
affect their women students. Only among men who teach in the
women's colleges is there a substantial positive response to these
issues. Women who teach in women's colleges rate themselves
fairly high in self-esteem. They represent about 45 percent of
the total faculty of such colleges. This means that women students in women's colleges are surrounded by the most woman-
supportive environment in higher education. Such a climate
comes closest to the climate available to men students in virtually
all other institutional settings. Unfortunately, however, 98 percent of women college students are enrolled in institutions where
the male-research-prestige model is preeminent. Only 2 percent of women students and about 10 percent of women who
receive baccalaureate degrees have had the benefits that normally accrue to men students. These important findings may be
related to earlier data showing that graduates of women's colleges are twice as likely to be cited for subsequent career achievement as women graduates of coeducational institutions.[3] Thus,

[3]M. E. Tidball, "Perspectives on Academic Women and Affirmative
Action," *Educational Record 54* (1973): 130–135.

there may be substantial losses of talent among women who attempt to develop cognitive and personal qualities in the generally unreceptive climate of coeducational institutions.

The demography, the self-esteem, the attitudes toward issues that affect women, and the relative values assigned to research and teaching provide a composite picture of the dominant themes in higher education. The profile of the successful teacher against whom we measure our own worth is that of a man from a Category I institution who accords little importance to teaching or woman-related issues and places his trust instead in research.

Men and research do not truly describe the nature of the academic profession. Nor can issues of equality be resolved so long as men and research dominate the academic scene. We followed the sputniks across the sky. They were political stars, but we mistook them for a signal to restructure higher education through the worship of science and technology. We forgot what we were about in our eager search for money at any price. But if it is valid to believe that the American system of higher education derives strength from diversity, and if diversity of institutional missions and contributions would be preserved, then the talents of women and the profession of teaching merit new affirmation and support, not only from educators but also from society.

22

In Pursuit of Equality: New Themes and Dissonant Chords

Eleanor Holmes Norton

A new equality has emerged during the past twenty years. It has been very much discussed but too little analyzed. It has been negatively associated with everything from the development of permissiveness to the demise of law and order. Its positive accreditations have sometimes been similarly exaggerated, as the use of the language of liberation to describe significant but modest moves toward equality suggests. This new equality has annoyed or exhilarated almost every part of our society, including higher education.

The emergence of black people out of the shadows as darkies and into the light as blacks is of course the throbbing center of the newest impulse toward equality. The nation is

still unraveling its oldest, most torturous, most redundant rid-
dle—the settlement of its black people. They alone among America's immigrants remain unsettled after 300 years. Over these
years they moved from slave plantations to rural hovels until
they emerged in the twentieth century as a profoundly urban
people still searching for their place in America. What changed
slowest about them was their status in America. In a land where
mobility seemed mandated and came to all but the damned,
America's dark-skinned immigrants remained at the bottom.
Only in the past two decades, beginning with the *Brown* decision,
has there been any serious challenge to the permanency of the
subterranean status of America's blacks and its other people
of color.

So elastic was the new equality that it readily stretched
to accommodate women, the nation's unequal majority. Following the pattern of the black revolution, women began rapidly
defining the meaning of equality for themselves and thus for
all of us in the 1970s. Should they fully succeed they could, by
the force of their numbers and the inherent radicalism of their
demands, cause society itself to make fundamental alterations.

But the open struggle of blacks for equality influenced
many more than those who saw themselves as similarly situated.
Most of the developments toward deeper equality took shape
and substance from the 1960s, a period characterized by the
upset of social convention and injustice. The sixties saw a deep
reaction to the spirit of the fifties which was a decade rooted more
in the notion that all men should be alike than that they should
be equal. The young people of the sixties were a quintessential
movement generation. The civil rights movement provided the
original social energy for this period. The antiwar movement,
the women's rights movement, the antipoverty movement, and
the struggles of other minorities all patterned themselves in
one fashion or another on the extraordinarily fertile civil rights
struggle.

Some changes that characterize the new equality appear
fairly permanent. The black struggle for equality has changed
America as much as it has changed the status of blacks. White
Americans today are the first white people in the nation's history
to be decisively influenced in their values by the experience,
aspirations, and actions of black Americans. Martin Luther

King, Jr., influenced America as much as did John F. Kennedy. Aretha Franklin and James Brown shaped the style of this period in the way that Dinah Shore and Bing Crosby influenced an earlier time.

Such changes in racial relations may be new, but they emerge from a special historic context. Historians may differ as to when to date the beginnings of the American obsession with equality, but the antislavery controversy of the Missouri Compromise surely marks a point when slavery, and thus equality, became truly national concerns tied to the destiny of the nation itself. At least since 1820, then, I think it fair to say that Americans have been locked in an unparalleled and unceasing struggle with themselves over the meaning and the virtue of equality.

For no other people has equality required such sustained attention for so long a time. Nowhere else in the world has the struggle over this single question been so intense, so dynamic, so costly. Over a period of 150 years it included not only the perplexing and omnipresent struggle of black men and women. For mounted on the same canvas are the collages of others, including the women's suffrage movement, the women's equality movement of today, and the largely successful struggle of European immigrants for inclusion on terms of equality and mobility. The very diversity of the actors who have played out equality themes in America has contributed to the preoccupation of Americans with this subject.

The American experience with equality has been both tortured and exhilarating. At the most promising end of the scale, successive waves of poor immigrants—most entering as illiterate peasants—found spectacular economic success in one or two generations, a phenomenal mobility unprecedented in world history. Somewhere in between are white women who, with the right to vote, won a new sense of themselves after a long struggle. While their transformation in equality terms is incomplete and disappointing, no one can doubt what the past fifty years have done to make the American woman more equal, both in her home and in her transformed rôle as member of the workforce. At the low end of the scale, the national experience with black people has been a unique tragedy, characterized first by sustained oppression and then by slow progress. Still, the past two decades have raised uncommon hopes and produced unprecedented gains. At the very least, black people have come up from psychological depths to which it would seem impossible to return.

Because Americans have had more diverse and concentrated experience with the dynamics of equality than any other people in the world, they have had the opportunity to disproportionately influence the very meaning of the word.

Examples of American leadership on matters of equality, leadership often carved out of painful experience, are legion. The choice of Martin Luther King, Jr., for world recognition as recipient of the Nobel Peace Prize in 1964 did not come because of his leadership of an indigenous freedom movement in the United States. King's world status derives from the same process that made world and not merely national leaders of Gandhi and Lenin. All staged essentially national movements with such universal force and applicability that they moved men and women across the face of the earth. King made the idea of racial equality plainer to millions than it had ever been before, just as Gandhi moved peasants everywhere to demand freedom from colonialism.

One could cite other examples of American pace-setting in defining equality. For example, the women's movement appears better developed in this country than in most others. Although France has a new cabinet post for the *condition feminine,* the country's notions of feminism are underdeveloped and there is no strong activist movement. Russian and other East European women have won significant access to male jobs but very little change in sex roles. By contrast, American women, with historically better developed concepts of equality to work with, are pursuing change in magnificent proportions from carefully circumscribed issues such as equal employment and universal child care to weighty philosophical issues whose resolution could virtually redefine womanhood and remake entire areas of human experience.

All of these developments toward greater equality in America have been influenced in no small measure by American higher education, both in its functional educational role and in its role as a social force. But the academic world, like most other sections of our society, is experiencing some difficulty to-

day, as pressure to implement the principles of equality has succeeded simple demand for common justice. New and more
complicated equality themes have replaced easier notions of
simple justice from the days of "Freedom Now."

I think it fair to say that in a very real sense the country
has traditionally depended on American higher education,
more than on most other institutions, for leadership on issues
of equality. But in recent years there have been some unchar-
acteristically discordant notes emanating from academe on
matters of equality that seem to challenge the applicability of
equality principles to the university setting. These arguments
have been made in such a way as to undermine the preeminent
place of the American university as a locus for pushing the society toward the realization of its own highest ideals.

I am not faulting academic voices for criticizing this or
that government approach to affirmative action in university
employment. There is much room for criticism. Moreover, the
university is in a position to offer the most useful criticism because of its own research and scholarly functions. Affirmative
action should not be exempt from criticism from academe simply because the university is affected. Rather, I would argue
just the opposite: that the academic community, which is in a
unique position to help perfect techniques for achieving equality, has inexplicably hung back from this natural function in
recent years. This lag can be seen both in areas where the university has some self-interest and in areas where it does not.

Let me cite just one area of neglect where university self-
interest is not implicated. Consider busing, a measure encoun-
tering deepening trouble and unpopularity throughout the
country. When James Coleman recently suggested that busing had spurred white flight from the cities and had thus hurt
school integration,[1] something of a furor developed. This deep-
ened when it was learned that the cities he had studied had indeed experienced white flight—but not busing.[2] Many who
believe in school integration now simply discount Coleman's

[1] P. Delaney, "Long-Time Desegregation Proponent Attacks Busing
as Harmful," *The New York Times,* June 7, 1975.
[2] I. Peterson, "Clark Group Assails New Coleman Study," *The New York Times,* June 25, 1975.

view as that of just one more renegade liberal adversary to integration. This, of course, is unfair to Coleman. Busing, like any controversial technique, needs criticism if we are to have any hope of making improvements. But in the context of today's chilled climate for racial equality, a finding that comes out of a decidedly negative context will only contribute to controversy. What is needed is not less criticism of the mechanisms of integration but more forthright searching for answers to complicated new issues that arise as we untangle our tortured racial past.

But when the thrust is one of complaint, rather than of searching, that a technique, busing for example, is not working, without suggesting an alternative, many hear only the sound of retreat. If not busing, what is proposed? In a country where racial degradation and separation have been the rule, few blacks are prepared to consider arguments based on the utility of various approaches to equality—not when whites have so often found the entire exercise of equality to be one of futility. This may not be a wholly rational response, but it is understandable. Coleman's conclusions concerning busing might have been received differently had they arisen within a more balanced study. But in the absence of a committed search for alternatives, civil rights advocates feel they will be a part of their own undoing if they acquiesce to doubts about busing or other integration techniques.

Who is in the best position to search for alternatives to this troublesome issue? Politicians, who find the issue especially treacherous in the political marketplace? The government, which feels the day-to-day pressure from both sides? Judges, sworn to expand constitutional principle and ignore popular reaction? None is in a better position than the university, where detachment and time are afforded to think through society's most difficult problems—from cures for diseases to school integration. How are we to account, therefore, for the scant study of the actual experience of children in integrated settings, except for the search for magical improvement in test scores, which many expected school integration to produce? There is even a danger that such promising techniques as the magnet school—one with special features designed to attract a balanced racial mix—will fail because no one has studied what specific features make such a school able to attract white students. I have seen some magnet schools thrown together so carelessly that they are bound to fail, giving the magnet concept a bad name as just one more failed integration technique. I have seen others that succeed and go unnoticed. One would think that some professor would be busily cataloging success and failure factors in magnet schools and by this time would be well on the way to developing a success model. In the absence of such assistance from the academic community, the New York Commission on Human Rights, hard pressed by budget cutbacks, is considering undertaking such a study to meet the urgent problems of school integration.

Busing is only one of a litany of issues produced by the new complexities of race, ethnicity, and sex in America where the need for thoughtful study is as clear as the neglect of scholarly attention. Two others among the most serious are the conflict between the values of seniority and affirmative action and the complicated question of how to encourage racially and economically diverse cities in the face of white flight, the flight of other middle-income people, and the resulting catastrophic effect on the viability of the American city itself. Both of these are issues on which the New York Commission on Human Rights, without a single Ph.D., has been struggling without federal or academic leadership.

Why problems of such magnitude have inspired so little academic attention is not altogether clear. But the failure of higher education to deal with issues of equality in the larger society does not help to create an affirmative and hospitable atmosphere once these issues come closer to home.

And they have come home to roost in academe on both faculty and student selection. Questions of faculty discrimination have provoked much more hostile reaction from administrators and faculty than have student selection matters, although the issues are at least of equal moment. The society has at least as great a stake in fair student selection as in fair faculty selection. Of course, the matter of self-interest is a bit clearer in one than in the other. In any case, the cries from college and university presidents and professors, almost all of them white men, have not been perceived by the public as disinterested laments.

I do not mean to imply that the objections of academicians are totally without merit. What I am saying is that universities have no right to ask for what amounts to an exemption from many of the procedures of the civil rights laws. To be sure, today most academic institutions have found their way toward a posture of compliance. But the early outcries, especially from the university presidents, called for a virtual exemption of colleges and universities from many of the only effective procedures that have been developed, all of which apply to every other large employer in the country. These techniques include an evaluation of confidential personnel records, a matter not without difficulty, but one also not beyond the reach of those interested in complying with the civil rights laws. Goals and timetables for rectifying exclusion within universities have also been subject to special displeasure. This issue, which continues to plow discord in academe, is also capable of resolution if compliance rather than avoidance is the goal.

The fact is that the blame for the way the controversy between the universities and the U.S. Department of Health, Education and Welfare (HEW) developed belongs with both sides. When compliance was first attempted, the universities responded like wounded deer, the victims of a predator that did not understand the sensitivity of the beast. Their traditional strong concern for equality was not summoned in this, their personal equality crisis. No galaxy of professors presented themselves as a technical task force to bring some reason into the process. The universities chose noncompliance until persistence by the federal government appeared to destroy that option.

For its own part, HEW, which had seen the face of recalcitrance before, identified this instance as just another garden variety. The agency was mindful that women professors had filed a massive class action against the entire university community to prod the department into a more forthright discharge of its antidiscrimination duties. In this atmosphere, the question of whether some serious work might be done by the department to adapt its procedures to college and university employment systems did not arise until negotiations were under way, often only after painful confrontation and then on an ad hoc rather than a systematic and comprehensive basis.

I believe it can be successfully argued that universities constitute a special case when it comes to antidiscrimination enforcement and that they need special assistance and perhaps even a system of race and sex analysis and implementation of remedies attuned to the peculiar contours of the university work place. As a technician with some experience in this field, I accept the view that factors that in other situations must be rigidly controlled, such as credentialism and broad discretion to evaluate a candidate, must have fuller sway in the selection of faculty. Moreover, I believe this need not lead to a more lenient application of the antidiscrimination laws to universities than to other employers, which would be a wholly unfair and unacceptable result.

By not looking at the university system as a particular case, HEW may have sown the seeds that have made enforcement so tough and controversial in colleges and universities. But if the government should have developed and provided better technical assistance to the universities, it was the universities themselves that should have been the richest resource for creating the appropriate technology. No other employer in the nation was in a position to influence government equal opportunity policy in the way the university was and is. By merely playing the role society expects of it, academe had the power to end the controversy over the procedures of compliance and, through research and scholarly study, to submit alternatives.

I am not suggesting that the university might have designed its own mode of compliance to equal opportunity laws. I am saying that by regarding the matter of compliance adversarily and not as an honest question of considerable technical difficulty, the university defaulted in its commitment to equality and encouraged needless and harmful controversy. No group of professors looked at these as serious questions for study. Instead, some formed themselves into a committee to oppose affirmative action. More recently, Nathan Glazer authored a book, *Affirmative Discrimination,* that purports to show that court decisions and other government actions to enforce the civil rights laws have themselves discriminated against the majority.[3] The deficiencies of this book begin with the author's failure to read and digest the relevant court decisions and to understand the basic law of remedies in our system of jurisprudence. Nowhere

---

[3]N. Glazer, *Affirmative Discrimination: Ethnic Inequality and Public Policy* (New York: Basic Books, 1975).

in all of corporate America, with its historic lack of identification with equality and association with prejudice, have developments so negative toward equality emerged to counter affirmative action.

Problems of equality in the university promise to multiply, not diminish, in the years ahead. While faculties doubled in the 1960s, with 30,000 new hires a year, in the 1980s only 6,000 new hires annually are expected, a replacement rate that itself may diminish as the years of fantastic expansion are followed not by stabilization but even by retrenchment. In February 1976 the National Center for Education Statistics published a report on the status of faculty women, stating that they lost ground in both salary increase and rank. According to the report, "The average salaries of men continue to exceed the average salaries of women at every academic rank and at every institutional level, in both publicly and privately controlled institutions."[4] If the university is to avoid becoming a haven for racial and sexual discord, it must summon its own best traditions, marshal its decided skill, and absorb itself in designing strategies for genuine equality.

In the same way student selection policies need urgent attention. If student admission procedures have upset administrators and professors less than faculty selection questions, they have been of considerable concern to society-at-large. Here, too, part of the blame rests squarely with government. Colleges and universities have been left almost totally to their own devices in designing techniques for the admission of disadvantaged minority students. The government encouraged the opening of opportunities but, as in the case of university affirmative action, provided no technical assistance.

The result was the *DeFunis* case and a number of others like it. These cases demonstrate that universities had more goodwill than expertise in evaluating disadvantaged minority students, who have been historically excluded from the student population. But even the goodwill has substantially diminished in the face of budgetary cutbacks and the controversy emanat-

[4]National Center for Education Statistics (Office of the Assistant Secretary of Education), *Salaries, Tenure and Fringe Benefits of Full-Time Instructional Faculty, 1975–76*, Preliminary Data (Washington, D.C.; U.S. Government Printing Office, February 4, 1976).

ing from these very cases. The problem will remain until someone considers it an issue worthy of serious research and study,
and who is in a better position than academicians to do this? But
neither the university nor the government has chosen to move
toward rational problem solving here either. Instead, court
cases continue to make this explosive issue even more explosive.
The adversary route has been chosen over the scholarly search.

The government is particularly at fault here, for there
has been a persuasive appeal for help on this matter before HEW
for almost two years. After the inconclusive Supreme Court
decision in the *DeFunis* case, I talked with the heads of six national racial and ethnic organizations, all with headquarters in
New York, who had been on opposite sides of the case. The
following letter (dated May 20, 1974) to then HEW Secretary
Caspar W. Weinberger resulted:

Dear Mr. Weinberger:
While the undersigned organizations have taken varying posi-
tions in the De Funis *case, we have over the years worked closely in*
support of civil rights and human freedom.
We all recognize that the process of creating affirmative action
is not an exact science. It is only in the past few years that the nation has
begun the development of procedures for dismantling discrimination.
All of us wish to avoid polarization. We agree that a primary
goal for all of us is the elimination of all forms of discrimination and the
establishment of affirmative actions and processes that will provide
equal opportunity within our constitutional framework.
Since the issues raised by the De Funis *case remain, we believe*
that an early response from HEW, within whose jurisdiction such mat-
ters lie, is indicated. We are therefore requesting that you direct the is-
suance of non-discriminatory guidelines clarifying how educational
institutions can best develop appropriate tools for special efforts to re-
cruit persons from previously excluded groups.

This letter was signed by the heads of the Anti-Defamation
League of B'nai Brith, the American Jewish Committee, the
American Jewish Congress, the NAACP, the National Urban League, and the Puerto Rican Legal Defense and Educational Fund.

Weinberger reacted immediately and a departmental
study and letter with guidelines to college and university presidents were promised. Over a year later, when Weinberger was

about to resign, I wrote to remind him that all were awaiting the promised guidance. I was assured that the matter would be carried on by his successor at HEW. Now almost another year has passed with no resolution of these issues.

This is inexcusable neglect from the federal government. The standards are theirs to give. Still, government default need not have been decisive. The knowledge and skills to develop fair admission devices are found in special abundance among various disciplines in the very universities that are now using similar resources to fight court cases. Once again academe has lost its way on issues that were thought to be its special concern.

In a very special way the country needs those who teach and administer higher education today. Rearrangements among the races and sexes and classes appear too complicated for many. The swirling events of our time seem to some not the inevitable content of modern change but a signal of endemic instability in American life. The line between dynamic change and perplexing instability has always been thin. But that line is not drawn entirely by events: It is drawn also by those who shape and react to events.

At such times, education is or should be a valuable hedge against bewilderment and panic. More than most Americans, educational leaders understand the reasons for the fear of change. After all, until the twentieth century most of the world's people lived virtually changeless lives. Change was a matter of the seasons or of youth mellowing into old age, which often came by forty. Change itself is a twentieth-century phenomenon. Change has made all our lives more difficult, but it has also made them more rewarding. We are richer but we are also more burdened.

I would be the first to agree that higher education cannot and should not always pursue the utilitarian. Academics are not society's annointed problem-solvers. But they have always ventured special concern for equality in America. It is time for them to step forward once again. Someone needs to stand with both reason and justice. If not the academic community, who?

Index

213